NATIONS of the WORLD

SAMUEL BRIMSON

Library of Congress Cataloging-in-Publication Data available
upon request from publisher. Fax (414) 336-0157 for the attention
of the Publishing Records Department.

ISBN 0-8368-5486-1

This North American edition first published in 2004 by
World Almanac® Library,
330 West Olive Street, Suite 100, Milwaukee, WI 53212 USA.

Created by Trocadero Publishing, an Electra Media Group
Enterprise, Suite 204, 74 Pitt Street, Sydney NSW 2000, Australia.

Original copyright © 2003 S. and L. Brodie.

WORLD ALMANAC® LIBRARY

Brazil

REPUBLIC OF BRAZIL

Brazil is the fifth largest country in the world. It occupies over three million square miles (appr. eight million sq km) and a major part of the continent of South America. Two distinct geographical regions make up most of Brazil. The vast Amazon basin spans the north, and the Planalto de Mato Grosso covers the center and south. The Amazon basin has the mighty Amazon River at its heart, with more than 1000 tributaries. Its landscape is dominated by rainforests growing in poor quality soils. Most of the inland plateau region is poor savannah woodland, while much of the northeast is scrubland. Better quality soils in the south sustain the coffee plantations so important to Brazil's economy.

The climate in Brazil varies according to location and altitude. Much of the country is tropical. The Amazon basin is hot and humid throughout the year, with regular heavy rainfall. In the northeast the São Francisco Basin is drier and subject to drought. Farther south the climate is variable, with warm to hot summers and cool to cold winters.

Almost eighty percent of Brazil's 165 million people live in urban areas. Most indigenous peoples, who account for less than one percent of the population, live in the Amazon Basin. Half the population are of Portuguese, Spanish, German and Italian descent. Twenty-five percent are of mixed ethnicity. There is even a tiny Japanese minority. Most Brazilians are Christian, with a minority of people who maintain animistic beliefs.

Brazil's official language is Portuguese. More than 120 languages are spoken by the indigenous population, mostly by small tribal groups. Close to one million people speak German, while just over half a million people speak Italian. Others speak Spanish, English or French.

Brazil is one of the world's major economies, and a dominant player in South America's overall economy. Economic mismanagement has brought difficult times for people and businesses in recent years. There is also a great disparity in the distribution of wealth. Land tends to belong to a small percentage of the population.

Agriculture plays a key role in Brazil's economic life. It is the world's largest producer and exporter of coffee. Brazilian orange juice pulp is exported in vast quantities around the world. Other important crops are bananas, sugar cane, soybeans, cacao, rice, corn and cotton. The production of beef cattle has grown substantially in recent decades. The clearing of rainforest to provide grazing lands has stirred worldwide controversy.

Brazil is the world's largest producer of iron ore. Other

FLAT EARTH PICTURE GALLERY

The spectacular geography of Rio de Janeiro.

The upper reaches of the Amazon River.

minerals extracted in large quantities include quartz, manganese, chrome ore, diamonds, nickel, tin, gold, bauxite, platinum and uranium. Steel, motor vehicles, ships, machinery, chemicals, textiles, footwear and processed foods are manufactured.

A federal republic of 26 states, Brazil operates under the constitution of 1988. The president is elected directly by the people and can serve two four-year terms. An appointed cabinet advises the president, who may intervene in national affairs at any time. The bicameral legislature consists of an upper house called the Senate and a lower house called the Chamber of Deputies. Senators are elected for eight year terms while deputies are elected for four years. Each state also has its own elected governor and legislature.

No written records of early Brazilian civilization exist. It is likely that people were dwelling in the region as long as 30,000 years ago. Archeologists have uncovered cave paintings which date back at least 11,000 years. The Arawaks and the Caribs were the two primary indigenous groups by the fifteenth century A.D. There was a total population of about one million people.

GOVERNMENT
Website www.brasil.gov.br
Capital Brasilia
Type of government Republic
Independence from Portugal
September 7, 1821
Voting
Universal compulsory adult suffrage
Head of state President
Head of government President
Constitution 1988
Legislature
Bicameral National Assembly
Chamber of Deputies (lower house),
Federal Senate (upper house)
Judiciary Supreme Federal Tribunal
Member of
IMF, OAS, UN, UNESCO, UNHCR,
WHO, WTO

LAND AND PEOPLE
Land area 3,300,171 sq mi
(8,547,404 sq km)
Highest point Pico da Neblina
9,765 ft (3,014 m)
Coastline 4,654 mi (7,491 km)
Population 176,029,560
Major cities and populations
São Paulo 19.5 million
Rio de Janeiro 5.7 million
Belo Horizonte 2.1 million
Ethnic groups European 50%,
Mulatto 22%, Mestizo 12%,
African 11%, indigenous 4%
Religions
Christianity 95%, Indigenous beliefs 4%
Languages
Portuguese, many indigenous languages

ECONOMIC
Currency Real
Industry
textiles, footwear, chemicals, cement,
timber, mining, steel, aircraft, motor
vehicles, machinery, food products
Agriculture
coffee, soybeans, wheat, rice, corn,
sugarcane, cocoa, citrus, beef
Natural resources
bauxite, gold, iron ore, manganese,
nickel, phosphates, platinum, tin,
uranium, petroleum, timber

Brazil

BRAND X PICTURES

Dutch West India Company exploited the lack of support the colony received from Spain. It took control of the entire northeast region with its profitable sugar plantations in 1633. The Company remained until 1654 when it was driven out by a Portuguese naval force sent from Rio de Janeiro.

Gold was discovered in the late seventeenth century, notably at Mina Gerais. This moved the economic balance of power away from the sugar-producing regions. Rio de Janeiro replaced Salvador as the Brazilian capital in 1763.

News of the revolutions in France and the American colonies sparked Brazilians' desire for independence. All attempts to establish a republic in the late eighteenth century were suppressed.

Portugal was over-run by Napoleon's armies and the monarchy was deposed in 1807. Portugal's King John VI fled to Brazil to create a new kingdom. Rio de Janeiro was the capital of Portugal's empire from 1808 to 1821. The kingdom of Brazil had equal status with that of Portugal.

When the monarch returned to Lisbon in 1821, he left his son Dom Pedro in Rio de Janeiro to rule as regent on his behalf. Dom Pedro declared

The first confirmed European sighting of the Brazilian coast was by Spanish explorer Vicente Yáñez Pinzón in the fifteenth century. Pedro Alvares Cabral claimed this vast region for Portugal in 1500. He named it after the red dyewood, paubrasil.

Thirty years later, under orders of King John III, Brazil was divided into 15 administrative regions called captaincies. They were to be developed to provide income for the colony. The first governor-general was Thome de Souza, who established a capital city at Salvador.

Portugal was under pressure to consolidate its hold on the vast region. Britain, Spain and France were all interested in this land.

For the rest of the sixteenth century, a sugar cane growing industry was developed in the northeast. Slave laborers were brought from Africa to work on the plantations. Many indigenous people captured in the inland regions were also sold into slavery.

When Portugal's throne was annexed by King Philip II of Spain, Brazil came under Spanish rule, from 1580 to 1640. The

The Cathedral da Se Nossa Senhora overlooks some classic examples of Portuguese colonial architecture.

himself Emperor of Brazil and the country independent on September 7, 1821. He abdicated ten years later after a failed war with Argentina.

A period of turmoil followed until Dom Pedro II came of age and was crowned in 1840. Brazil now entered a golden age of development. Its new wealth depended largely on Europe's huge demand for Brazilian coffee.

World opinion had been turning against slavery. Britain abolished it in 1834. Many of Brazil's people demanded similar action. Terrified of the economic consequences, sugar planters opposed the abolition

movement. When coffee planters joined the campaign in 1888, slavery was banned. Angry sugar planters joined forces with republicans to stage a coup d'état. Emperor Dom Pedro was deposed in 1889.

The new Republic of Brazil produced its first constitution in 1891, with Marshal Manuel Deodoro da Fonesca as president. Economic growth continued. In addition to the coffee boom, world demand for rubber was growing steadily. The rubber boom ended in the early twentieth century, when rubber plants smuggled out of Brazil were established in Southeast Asia.

Brazil's reliance on a continuing demand for coffee was behind the coup d'état staged in 1930 by Getúlio Vargas. He centralized many functions of

the government and laid the basis for a more industrialized Brazil. During the 1930s, however, he increasingly favored the powerful landowners against the rest of society. Harsh security legislation was introduced to please the military. This culminated in the creation of the New State in 1937. It was modelled on European fascism, with Vargas as dictator.

Tthe military forced Vargas' resignation, replacing him with General Eurico Gaspar Dutra in 1945. He ruled until 1950 when Vargas returned as the elected president. The following years were marked by a weak economy and consistent political distress. Vargas committed suicide shortly after resigning office in 1954.

Juscelino Kubitchek became president in the election the following year. He granted major economic concessions

Brazilian tropical fruits on sale in Olinda.

to foreign investors. They built factories to manufacture cars, chemicals and electrical goods.

Kubitchek also exploited Brazilian national pride by constructing a new capital city called Brasilia in just three years. The foreign loans used to finance it brought hardship to the national economy.

Kubitchek's conservative successor, Jânio da Silva Quadros, was a surprise to his backers. He embarked on an independent foreign policy aimed at reducing Brazil's dependence on the United States. He also backed the communist revolution in Cuba, among other radical moves in the region.

After just one year Quadros was replaced by João Goulart, whose powers were curtailed by the congress. Presidential powers were restored in 1963, but Goulart was deposed in a United States-backed coup d'é-tat the following year. The government of the country then passed to two political parties, both controlled by the military.

For the next ten years Brazil endured a regime of increasing brutality at the hands of the armed forces. Thousands who defied bans on political activity and the organization of labor were imprisoned and tortured. The generals actively sought foreign investment, however, and vast sums of money flowed into the country.

The 1973 oil crisis hit Brazil very hard. It was heavily dependent on imported oil. The enormous sums it owed international financial organizations rapidly escalated, making Brazil the world's largest debtor nation. Despite this, the years from 1979 to 1985 were marked by rapid economic growth.

Quasi-military rule finally ended in 1985 when José Sar-ney became president. He helped enact a new constitution calling for the direct election of the president in 1988. In 1990, when people voted in the first truly democratic manner, Fernando Collor de Mello was elected president. However, within two years he faced impeachment on charges of corruption. Although cleared in 1994 he was barred from resuming the role of president.

Fernando Henrique Cardoso took office in January 1995. He reduced state control of the economy and privatized government-owned energy and communications companies. A new currency helped bring the rampant inflation under control. Progress was made in redistributing land from large landowners to the poor.

Cardoso was reelected in 1998. He was forced to negotiate a U.S.$42 billion financial package with the International Monetary Fund. The stringent economic plan this involved led to increased investor confidence. By 1999 the situation had stabilized. Strong economic growth of the early 2000s helped continue the positive trend. Unfortunately, members of the Cardoso government continue to face allegations of drug trafficking.

A statue of Jesus Christ high on the mountains above Rio de Janeiro.

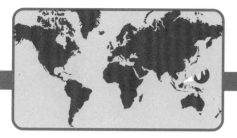

Brunei

ISLAMIC SULTANATE OF BRUNEI

GOVERNMENT

Website www.brunei.gov.bn
Capital Bandar Seri Begawan
Type of government
Absolute monarchy
Independence from Britain
January 1, 1984
Voting None
Head of state Sultan
Head of government Sultan
Constitution 1959, partially
suspended
Legislature
Unicameral Legislative Council,
appointed by Head of State
Judiciary Supreme Court
Member of APEC, ASEAN, CN,
IMF, UN, WHO, WTO

LAND AND PEOPLE
Land area 2,226 sq mi
(5,765 sq km)
Highest point Bukit Pagon
5994 ft (1850 m)
Coastline 100 mi (161 km)
Population 350,898
Major cities and populations
Bandar Seri Begawan 52,000
Ethnic groups
Malay 80%, Chinese 20%
Religions
Islam 75%, Buddhism 15%,
Christianity 10%
Languages
Malay(official), English, Chinese

ECONOMIC
Currency Bruneian dollar
Industry
petroleum, petroleum refining,
natural gas
Agriculture
rice, vegetables, fruits, poultry
Natural resources
petroleum, natural gas, timber

Oil-rich Brunei faces the South China Sea on the northeastern coast of the island of Borneo. The landscape varies from swampland on the coast to hilly rainforests in the interior. Seventy five percent of the land is heavily forested. The climate is tropical with high temperatures and humidity throughout the year.

Most Bruneins are Malays. About twenty percent are Chinese. Indigenous peoples inhabit the inland rainforests. Islam is the state religion. Most people are Sunni Muslims, while fifteen percent are Buddhists and ten percent are Christian. Malay is the official language, but English and Chinese are also spoken.

Brunei was trading with China in the sixth century A.D. By the fourteenth century it was controlled by the Hindu Majapahit Empire, based in Java to the south. It grew into a key port for northern Borneo.

Brunei became an independed sultantate, occupying the entire island of Borneo and many surrounding islands in the early fifteenth century. By the nineteenth century, the coastline had become a haven for pirates. The sultan of Brunei gave the region of Sarawak to British adventurer James Brooke as a reward for ridding his country of those pirates. The sultan responded positively to Britain's ongoing offer of protection. In 1888, Brunei became a British protectorate.

Japan invaded Brunei during World War II, prompted by the country's rich oil reserves. Britain returned control to the sultan at the end of the war.

A written constitution was proclaimed in 1959. A partially elected Legislative Council was established three years later.

In 1963, Malaya proposed a union of Singapore, Sabah, Sarawak and Brunei as a new nation called the Federation of Malaysia. Widespread opposition led to riots in Brunei. Sultan Omar Ali Saifuddien suspended the constitution and dissolved the Legislative Council. The formation of Malaysia proceeded without Brunei. British control continued.

The British government signed a new treaty with Muda Hassanal, the sultan of Brunei, in 1979. Brunei became fully independent on January 1, 1984. Political parties were banned. The sultan rules by decree, taking advice from an appointed council. Any dissent is firmly suppressed. The sultan is one of the world's wealthiest people, primarily because of the country's oil reserves. He is descended from the family which has ruled the land for six centuries. Brunei has one of the highest per capita gross domestic products in Southeast Asia.

Bulgaria

REPUBLIC OF BULGARIA

The Republic of Bulgaria is located in southeastern Europe. Running east to west across the center of the country are the Balkan Mountains. The beautiful, fertile Danube River plains lie north of these mountains. The Rhodope Mountains create a natural southern border with Greece. The southern climate is Mediterranean, with hot summers and mild winters. Farther north, winter temperatures are much lower.

Seventy percent of the population lives in cities or towns. Eighty percent of the people are Bulgars and ten percent are Turkish. There are significant Gypsy and Macedonian minorities. The Christian Eastern Orthodox and Armenian Apostolic religions are practiced by eighty percent of the people. Around twelve percent are Sunni Muslims.

The main language is Bulgarian, which is closely related to Serbo-Croat, Slovene and Russian. It also adopted various aspects of Turkish, Albanian and Greek as it developed. Minority languages include Romany and Turkish.

Manufacturing industries include machinery, metal works, engineering, electronics, textiles, chemicals and food processing. Copper, zinc, coal, bauxite, lead, natural gas, oil and iron ore are extensively mined. Farms produce wheat, barley, vegetables, tobacco, oilseeds and corn.

Bulgaria is a parliamentary republic. The president is elected by the people. The unicameral National Assembly has 240 members elected by proportional representation. The prime minister leads these legislators. The current constitution was adopted in 1991.

Around 3500 B.C., Thracians migrated from the Eurasian steppes to what is now Bulgaria. During the fourth century B.C., they were conquered by Macedonia and subsequently by the Roman Empire. The region was devastated by invasions between the third and sixth centuries A.D. The Bulgars, of mixed Slav and Turkic descent, arrived in the fifth

The walls of the ancient Tsaravets Citadel at Veliko Tarnovo.

century. They converted to Christianity in the late ninth century.

Following centuries of independence, Bulgaria fell to the Turkish Ottoman Empire in the late 1300s. The determined Bulgarians made many attempts to overthrow the Turks during the next 500 years. After one such attempt in 1876, the Turks responded by killing more than 15,000 Bulgarian men, women, and children.

When the Turks were defeated in the Russo-Turkish War of 1877–78, they lost control of most of Bulgaria. Then its boundaries were re-drawn at the insistence of Austria-Hungary and Britain. Prince Ferdinand of Saxe-Coburg-Gotha became king in 1887. The country gained independence on October 5, 1908. Ferdinand became czar.

Bulgaria defeated Turkey in the 1911–12 Balkan War but failed to gain control of Macedonia. This prompted Bulgaria to support Germany and Austria-Hungary in World War I.

Political instability in the 1920s was followed by the economic hardship of the Depression in 1930. Kimon Georgiev became prime minister, with military help, in 1934. He suspended constitutional government. A year later Czar Boris III took personal control of the country, ruling as a dictator.

In 1941, Germany pressured Bulgaria to join the Axis powers in World War II. Although allied with Germany, Czar Boris refused to persecute Bulgarian Jews. When the Soviet military took Bulgaria in September 1944, the government was reorganized under their Fatherland Front.

Bulgaria was declared a people's republic in 1946. Communist leader Georgi Dimitrov became Prime Minister. After his death three years later, Todor Zhivkov took over leadership.

A brutal campaign of Bulgarization of the population took place in the 1980s. The Turkish language was banned and 800,000 ethnic Turks were forced to take Bulgarian names. Zhikov was deposed in 1989.

Elected in August 1990, Zheliu Zhelev was the first non-communist leader since 1944. A new constitution took effect the following year.

Bulgaria's economy suffered dramatically during the 1990s. Economic reforms begun in the 1980s have been only slightly` successful. A Socialist Party candidate was elected in 2001.

In 2001, Bulgaria offered the use of an air corridor for American troops in an anti-terrorist operation in Afghanistan. Shortly afterward, Bulgaria was elected as a non-permanent member of the United Nations Security Council.

GOVERNMENT
Website www.government.bg
Capital Sofia
Type of government Republic
Independence from Ottoman Empire October 5, 1908
Voting Universal adult suffrage
Head of state President
Head of government Prime Minister
Constitution 1991
Legislature Unicameral National Assembly
Judiciary Supreme Administrative Court
Member of IMF, NATO, UN, UNESCO, WHO, WTO

LAND AND PEOPLE
Land area 42,855 sq mi (110,994 sq km)
Highest point Musala 9,478 mi (2,925 m)
Coastline 221 mi (354 km)
Population 7,621,337
Major cities and populations
Sofia 1,200,000
Plovdiv 390,000
Varna 325,000
Burgas 210,000
Ethnic groups Bulgar 80%, Turkish 10%,
Religions Christianity 80%, Islam 12%
Languages Bulgarian (official)

ECONOMIC
Currency Lev
Industry electricity, gas, food, wine, machinery, chemical products, coke, refined petroleum, nuclear fuel
Agriculture vegetables, fruits, livestock, wheat, barley, sunflowers, beet sugar
Natural resources bauxite, copper, lead, zinc, coal, timber

Burkina Faso

PEOPLE'S REPUBLIC OF BURKINA FASO

Landlocked Burkina Faso is located in western Africa. south of the Sahara Desert. Its lies on a vast plateau covered with grasslands, small trees and low hills. Soils are of poor quality and rainfall is varied but infrequent. In the harsh climate daytime temperatures average 80°F (26°C).

Burkina Faso has as many as fifty ethnic groups. The Mossi account for half of the population. Sixty-five percent of the people follow traditional animist religions, while Muslims and Christians make up significant minorities. French is the official language but many other languages are spoken. Due to underdevelopment and poverty, less than twenty percent of the people are literate.

The region was inhabited by Bobo, Lobi and Gurunsi ethnic groups in the twelfth century A.D. They were displaced a century later by Mossi invaders from the south. Combining religious teachings and good management, the Mossi retained control until colonial times.

France incorporated the region into French West Africa near the end of the nineteenth century. The name Upper Volta was adopted in 1920. Twelve years later, control was divided among French Soudan, Niger and the Ivory Coast. By 1947, Upper Volta was made a separate administrative unit with limited French control.

Upper Volta declined to join the proposed nation of West Africa. It was granted independence on August 5, 1960. President Maurice Yaméogo quickly imposed a one-party state. He was deposed by the military in 1966. A new constitution in 1970 brought a partial return to civilian rule.

The army took control again in 1983, bringing Captain Thomas Sankara to power. He focused on economic development and renamed the nation Burkina Faso in 1984.

After Sankara's assassination in 1987, Captain Blaise Compaoré took power. Compaoré was elected president the following year under the 1991. He has been reelected twice since.

Burkina Faso remains a very poor nation. In the early 2000s, both the World Bank and the International Monetary Fun made large grants to the country for food, water, and medicines.

The country is known to have large deposits of manganese and gold, as well as smaller resources in other precious metals. It is hoped that mining industries can be developed in order to decrease the country's dependence upon farming. For a nation which receives so little rainfall and has limited access to fresh water, little economic security lies in farm income.

GOVERNMENT
Website www.primature.gov.bf
Capital Ouagadougou
Type of government Republic
Independence from France
August 5, 1960
Voting Universal adult suffrage
Head of state President
Head of government Prime Minister
Constitution 1991
Legislature
Unicameral National Assembly
Judiciary Supreme Court
Member of IMF, OAU, UN, UNESCO, WHO, WTO

LAND AND PEOPLE
Land area 105,946 sq mi
(274,400 sq km)
Highest point Tena Kourou
2,427 ft (749 m)
Population 12,603,185
Major cities and populations
Ouagadougou 1 million
Bobo-Dioulasso 450,000
Ethnic groups
Mossi 50%, others 50%
Religions
Traditional animism 65%, Islam
25%, Christianity 10%
Languages
French (official), indigenous
languages

ECONOMIC
Currency CFA franc
Industry
cotton lint, beverages, agricultural
processing, soap, textiles, mining
Agriculture
peanuts, sesame, cotton, sorghum,
millet, corn, rice, livestock
Natural resources
manganese, limestone, marble,
antimony, copper, nickel, bauxite,
lead, phosphates, zinc, silver

Burundi

REPUBLIC OF BURUNDI

GOVERNMENT
Capital Bujumbura
Type of government Republic
Independence from Belgium (UN Trust Territory) Ju;y 1, 1962
Voting Universal adult suffrage
Head of state President
Head of government President
Constitution 1998
Legislature
Bicameral Parliament
National Assembly (lower house),
Senate (upper house)
Judiciary Supreme Court
Member of IMF, OAU, UN,
UNESCO, WHO, WTO

LAND AND PEOPLE
Land area 10,740 sq mi
(27,816 sq km)
Highest point
Mount Heha 8,942 ft (2,760 m)
Population 6,373,000
Major cities and populations
Bujumbura 350,000
Gitega 105,000
Ethnic groups
Hutu 84%, Tutsi 15%, Twa 1%
Religions
Christianity 70%, traditional
animism 30%
Languages
French, Kirindi (both official)

ECONOMIC
Currency Burundi franc
Industry
consumer goods, component
assembly, food processing
Agriculture
coffee, cotton, tea, corn, sorghum,
sweet potatoes, bananas, tapioca,
beef, dairy, hides
Natural resources
nickel, uranium, rare earth oxides,
peat, cobalt, copper, platinum,
vanadium

Burundi is in central Africa, near the equator. It sits on a high plateau with mountains to the west. The western section of the Great Rift Valley passes through Burundi. The climate is equatorial, with distinct wet and dry seasons.

The Hutu people account for more than eighty percent of the population. Most others are Tutsi. Two-thirds of the people are Christian. Many still follow traditional animist beliefs. French and Kirindi are the official languages. Almost eighty percent of the people can read and write.

The Twa were the original inhabitants of the region. By the fourteenth century A.D. the Hutu were displacing them. The Tutsi established dominance over the Hutu within the next hundred years. Soon the the Hutu were relegated to tending Tutsi cattle.

Germany claimed Burundi in the 1880s, combining it with Ruanda (now Rwanda) to make up German East Africa. Following World War I, under a League of Nations mandate, Belgium controlled the colony called Ruanda-Urundi. It was made a U. N. trust territory after World War II. Burundi became an independent constitutional monarchy on July 1, 1962.

Ongoing rivalry between theTutsi and Hutu caused consistent bloodshed as each group fought for control. Tutsi ruler Mwambutsa IV was deposed by his son Ntare in 1966. He was in turn overthrown by the military. Tutsi Captain Michel Micombero seized control and declared Burundi a republic. In additional coups, the Tutsi remained in power. Ethnic violence in the late 1980s left 5,000 people dead.

Melchior Ndadaye, the first Hutu president, was elected in 1993. He was deposed and killed by Tutsi military forces. More that 150,000 people were killed in ethnic fighting during the next few years.

President Cyprien Ntaryamira, another Hutu leader, died in a suspicious aircraft crash in 1994. A subsequent power- sharing arrangement collapsed and ethnic bloodshed continued. A third Hutu, Sylvestre Ntibantuganya, was overthrown in 1996. The army named Pierre Buyoya president. Uganda, Kenya and Tanzania applied economic sanctions in protest to the takeover.

Nelson Mandela was appointed by a group of African nations as a mediator in 2000. The Tutsi-led government and most of the Hutu rebel groups signed a peace agreement at that time. Some peace has been achieved, but Hutu rebel offensives continue. A coup attempt by junior army officers was put down in April of 2001.

Cambodia

KINGDOM OF CAMBODIA

Cambodia shares the Indochina Peninsula with Laos and Vietnam. The Dangrek and Cardamom Mountain ranges form its western boundaries. The center of the country is a fertile plain through which the Mekong River flows. The climate is tropical, with heavy rains between May and September. The average annual temperature is about 80 F. (26.7°C.).

Cambodia has fewer people per square mile than most other countries of Southeast Asia. Around ninety percent of its people are ethnic Khmers. The rest are Chinese, Vietnamese or hill tribespeople. Ninety percent of the people are Theravada Buddhists. There are small numbers of Christians and some Muslims. The official language is Khmer, but many people speak French.

Funan was established as a state in what is now Cambodia in the first century A.D., extending southeast along the Mekong River valley. India introduced the Hindu religion and a new legal system in the fourth century A. D.

Chenla, home of the Khmers in the northeast, conquered Funan in the sixth century A.D. Three-hundred years later Prince Jayavarman incorporated Funan and Chenla into his Angkor Empire. Its great legacy was the stunning Angkor Wat temple complex.

Jayavarman II expanded the empire substantially in the eleventh century. He incorporated Cambodia, Siam, Laos, Vietnam and parts of Malaya. The kingdom declined in the 1200s. Eventually much of it fell to the Ayutthaya Empire of Siam (Thailand). Other parts went to Annam, in present-day Vietnam.

France forced Khmer King Norodom to accept its protection in 1863. Cambodia was annexed as a full colony the next year. It became part of the Union of Indochina in 1887. During World War II, Japan occupied Cambodia.

Eighteen-year-old Norodom Sihanouk became king.

Cambodia became internally self-governing after France's return in 1946. Cambodians were discontent under the control of France. The people gained independence in 1953 under the leadership of Sihanouk. Vietnamese communist forces occupied the country the following year. They soon retreated without causing any harm to the Sihanouk government.

Sihanouk gave up the throne in favor of his father in 1955. The younger Sihanouk wanted to become more active in politics. As a prince, he spent time visitng other countries to encourage new development in Cambodia. He made every

The Silver Pagoda royal palace in Phnom Penh.

FLAT EARTH PICTURE GALLERY

FLAT EARTH PICTURE GALLERY

Human skulls, victims of the Pol Pot era, in the Stupa Choeng Ek memorial.

The country was renamed Democratic Kampuchea. Much of the population was forced to work on the land. Modern technology, seen as a symbol of western influence, was destroyed. The Khmer Rouge killed more than 1.5 million Cambodians.

Vietnam deposed the Khmer Rouge in 1978. Guerrilla units continued a campaign of harassment. A new republic was established under the leadership of Hun Sen. Following peace talks in Paris, Vietnam withdrew its forces in 1989.

A United Nations peace treaty was signed in 1991. It stated that the U. N., working with Cambodian and opposition leaders, would establish a new government. Elections were held in 1993. Norodom Sihanouk returned as king with his son Ranariddh and Hun Sen as co-premiers.

The Khmer Rouge continued its guerrilla activities. It split into two groups, one of which agreed to peace terms. Pol Pot died in 1998 and his movement collapsed.

A coup by Hun Sen in 1997 led to conflict with factions controlled by Ranariddh. Hun Sen won a disputed election in 1998 and became sole premier. Ranariddh continues to be a prominent opposition leader.

effort to keep Cambodia out of the Vietnam War.

Lieutenant General Lon Nol led a coup d'état against the king in 1970. Sihanouk established a government-in-exile in Beijing. Supported by South Vietnam and the United States, Cambodia began expelling communist forces. Brutal actions by the South Vietnamese strengthened Cambodian support for the Khmer Rouge communists.

Cambodia became the Khmer Republic on October 9,1970. The Khmer Rouge now controlled two-thirds of the nation. Lon Nol's government resorted to a desperate crackdown, which only aided the communists. Pol Pot's Khmer Rouge overthrew the Lon Nol government in 1975.

GOVERNMENT
Website www.cambodia.gov.kh
Capital Phnom Penh
Type of government Constitutional monarchy
Independence from France November 9, 1953
Voting Universal adult suffrage
Head of state Monarch
Head of government Prime Minister
Constitution 1993
Legislature Bicameral Parliament National Assembly (lower house), Senate (upper house)
Judiciary Supreme Council of the Magistracy
Member of ASEAN, IMF, UN, UNESCO, WHO

LAND AND PEOPLE
Land area 69,898 sq mi (181,035 sq km)
Highest point Phnum Aoral 5,864 ft (1,810 m)
Coastline 276 mi (443 km)
Population 12,775,324
Major cities and populations Phnom Penh 975,000 Battambang 200,000
Ethnic groups Khmer 90%, others 10%
Religions Buddhism 90%, Islam 3%, others 7%
Languages Khmer (official), French

ECONOMIC
Currency Riel
Industry tourism, rice milling, fishing, timber products, rubber, cement, mining, textiles, garments
Agriculture rice, rubber, corn, vegetables
Natural resources timber, gemstones, manganese, phosphates

Cameroon

REPUBLIC OF CAMEROON

Cameroon is a small republic in western Africa. A narrow plain of swampland and rainforest runs along its Atlantic coast. Mount Cameroon, a 13,350 feet (4,069 m) high volcano, is located just inland. The north is mainly thickly forested plateau, giving way to savannah. Cameroon, one of the wettest countries on earth, has a tropical climate.

The Fang, Bamileke and Bamum are the largest of Cameroon's 200 ethnic groups, forming forty percent of the population. Also significant are the Douala, Luanda, Bassa, Fulani, Tikar, and Mandara.

Animist faiths are practiced by many people, while others are Christians and Muslims. In addition to English and French, over twenty different African languages are spoken. Half of Cameroon's people are literate.

Bantu-speaking tribes lived in Cameroon around 1000 B.C. Over the next centuries the Fang, Kanuri, Hausa and Fulani arrived, pushing indigenous forest dwellers south.

The Portuguese reached the Wuori River in 1472, naming it Rio dos Camarõs, from which Cameroon got its name. Many native people were captured and pressed into slavery. Duoala chiefs signed an agreement with Germany in 1884.

Trade of palm oil, ivory, cacao and rubber developed as Germany built roads and rail lines. Because of this development, France and Britain invaded the area during World War I.

The League of Nations placed Cameroon under joint British-French control after the war. In 1945, the United Nations gave western Cameroon to Britain and eastern Cameroon to France. An independence and reunification movement launched guerrilla actions during the 1950s. French Cameroon became independent in 1960, with Ahmadou Ahidjo as president. Part of northern British Cameroon became Nigeria while the south joined Cameroon the next year.

Cameroon became a one-party state. Tough economic reforms by Ahidjo's successor, Paul Biya, provoked a 1984 coup attempt. The oil industry has brought a degree of prosperity to the nation since the 1970s. International groups are working to bring more of that income to the poor.

Biya permitted opposition political movements following national strikes in 1990. Two years later he was elected president. Biya won again in 1997 when opposition parties boycotted the election due to claims of widespread voting fraud.

GOVERNMENT
Capital Yaoundé
Type of government Republic
Independence from France (UN Trust Territory) January 1, 1960
Voting Universal adult suffrage
Head of state President
Head of government Prime Minister
Constitution 1972, revised 1996
Legislature Unicameral National Assembly
Judiciary Supreme Court
Member of IMF, OAU, UN, UNESCO, WHO, WTO

LAND AND PEOPLE
Land area 183,569 sq mi (475,442 sq km)
Highest point 13,268 ft (4,095 m)
Coastline 251 mi (402 km)
Population 16,184,748
Major cities and populations
Douala 1.3 million
Yaoundé 1.1 million
Ethnic groups
Fang 20%, Bamileke 18%, Duala 15%, Fulani 10%, others 37%
Religions Traditional animism 40%, Christianity 40%, Islam 20%
Languages
French, English (both official), indigenous languages

ECONOMIC
Currency CFA franc
Industry
oil refining, mining, food processing, consumer goods, textiles, timber
Agriculture
coffee, cacao, cotton, rubber, bananas, oilseed, grains, livestock, timber
Natural resources
petroleum, bauxite, iron ore, timber

Canada

GOVERNMENT
Website canada.gc.ca
Capital Ottawa
Type of government
Federal parliamentary democracy
Independence from Britain
1 July 1867 (dominion status)
Voting Universal adult suffrage
Head of state
British Crown,
represented by Governor-General
Head of government Prime Minister
Constitution 1867, 1982
Legislature
Bicameral Parliament
House of Commons (lower house),
Senate (upper house)
Judiciary Supreme Court
Member of APEC, CN, G-10, IMF,
NAFTA, NATO, OAS, OECD, UN,
UNESCO, UNHCR, WHO, WTO

LAND AND PEOPLE
Land area 3,558,084 sq mi (9,215,430
sq km)
Highest point Mount Logan
19,307 ft (5959 m)
Population 31,902,268
Major cities and populations
Toronto 4.5 million
Montreal 3.5 million
Vancouver 2.0 million
Ottawa-Hull 1.1 million
Ethnic groups Caucasian 92%,
indigenous 2%, others 6%,
Religion Christianity 90%,
Languages English, French (both
official), indigenous languages

ECONOMIC
Currency Canadian dollar
Industry
motor vehicles, mining, chemicals,
minerals processing, food products,
wood products, paper products; fishing,
petroleum, natural gas, tourism
Agriculture wheat, barley, oilseed,
fruits, vegetables; dairy, timber, seafood
Natural resources
iron ore, nickel, zinc, copper, gold, lead,
molybdenum, potash, silver, seafood,
timber, coal, petroleum, natural gas

The second-largest country in the world, Canada occupies more than forty percent of the North American continent. It is bounded by the United States as well as the Atlantic, Arctic, and Pacific Oceans.

The landscape includes lowlands around Hudson Bay and the St Lawrence–Great Lakes region. Much of this area is taken up by the vast Canadian Shield, a granite plateau covered with only a thin layer of soil. The plains of Manitoba and Saskatchewan are the northern end of the prairie lands of the United States. Rugged mountains and highlands line the east coast. The Canadian Cordillera, a massive mountain range, stretches from the Yukon to the border with the United States on the west.

Canada's climate is characterized by long and cold winters. Conditions in the far north are polar. The southernmost region is temperate with summers often achieving high temperatures. The warmest part of the country is the west, around Vancouver.

The population is cosmopolitan. People from almost every part of the world make their homes in Canada. At least seventy-five percent live in urban areas. The most obvious ethnic difference is between Canadians of British and French descent. About forty percent are from a British background, twenty seven percent are from French. Many people claim both British and French ancestry. At least ten percent of all Canadians have Asian backgrounds, predominantly Chinese and Vietnamese. Other ethnic groups include Ukrainian, Italian, German and Dutch. Just over one percent of the population is aboriginal or mixed aboriginal and European. The original inhabitants of the northwest are the Inuit, many of whom live a traditional lifestyle.

There is complete freedom of worship in Canada. About ninety percent of the population is Christian. The balance is made up by minority groups of Jews, Muslims, Buddhists and Hindus.

Canada is officially bilingual, with English and French as the official languages. All official documents are published in both languages. Language use tends to split along geographical lines. The Quebec province is a stronghold of French usage, while other provinces are primarily English-speaking. Indigenous peoples use various Amerindian languages which vary from region to region.

Manufacturing, agriculture, mining and services form the core of Canada's economy. Wheat is a key crop for domestic consumption and export across the world. It is grown

Canada

The CN Tower dominates the Toronto skyline.

on vast tracts of land in Manitoba, Saskatchewan and Alberta. The raising of beef cattle is also important in these regions, and in Ontario. Apples and peaches are the main fruits harvested in Canada. More than half the land mass is forested, making timber a major industry. Seafood, particularly salmon and lobster, is a large export earner.

Manufactured goods include transportation equipment, processed foods, chemicals, metal products, petroleum, paper products, motor vehicles, electronic products, wood products and clothing. Much of Canada's industry is foreign-owned, mostly by United States interests. This leaves the country vulnerable to conditions over which it has no control. The situation has been eased by the North America Free Trade Agreement (NAFTA). It has encouraged Canadian companies to invest in the United States.

Huge amounts of zinc, nickel, uranium, lead, tantalum and cobalt are mined in Canada. Almost as important are oil and natural gas, iron ore, coal, silver, diamonds, copper and sulphur. The mineral extraction industries would be larger if so many of Canada's mineral deposits

were not under ice or snow much of the year.

Services and tourism are also major earners for the economy. About sixty-five percent of the Canadian gross domestic product comes from service industries. Spectacular scenery and relative safety make Canada a major attraction for tourists. The rise of the multicultural society has also contributed to an increase in visitor numbers.

Canada is a constitutional monarchy. The British monarch, as head of state, is represented in Canada by the governor-general. The national government is based in Ottawa, the capital city, with a bicameral parliament. The lower house is the House of Commons, the upper house is the Senate. Commons members are elected from single member electorates based on population. Senators are elected on a provincial basis. The head of government is the prime minister, who holds office with the support of the House of Commons. Elections are held every five years. Each of the provinces has its own parliament with elected members, headed by a premier.

Most archeologists believe that Canada's first inhabitants arrived from Asia, possibly migrating by sea or across land over what is now the Bering Strait. These were the ancestors of indigenous peoples such as the Algonquin, Iroquois and Huron. Inuit tribes settled in the harsh climate of the Arctic area.

Many believe that Scandinavian Leif Ericson was the first European to reach the area in about A.D. 1000. Archeologists have found evidence of various short-lived settlements on the east coast about that time.

British explorer John Cabot landed on the east coast in 1497, followed in 1534 by Frenchman Jacques Cartier. Neither had much interest in the land itself. Most explorers were seeking a northwest sea passage which would take them to Asia. Cartier did claim the St. Lawrence area for France.

The first permanent settlements were built beginning in 1605. French fur traders established a base in Nova Scotia and another at Quebec City. Thus began the steady disruption of native cultures by the colonists of New France. Explorer Samuel de Champlain developed a working relationship with the Algonquins and Hurons. This merely created further disputes with the Iroquois.

The British built settlements south of the French outposts about the same time. France and Britain were in conflict over continued access to the lucrative fur trade by the late seventeenth century.

The French and Indian War, which began in 1754, saw France and Britain fighting for control of Canada. France was forced to relinquish its Quebec settlement when it was defeated. New France was now a possession of Britain. Controlling it was no simple task. Large numbers of French settlers dominated the commercially vital St. Lawrence River. Britain passed the Quebec Act of 1774, which recognized the Catholic Church and the French language, to satisfy these settlers.

The American Revolution, from 1775 to 1783, changed the face of Canada. When Britain lost the American colonies, thousands of loyalists fled north to Canada. Having lost their property during the revolution, they maintained a bitter anti-American outlook. This prompted the United States to invade Canada during the war of 1812. The conflict finally ended with Britain and the United States defining the border between the two countries.

The formerly Catholic French colony had now been overrun by Protestant English. London soon became concerned about the friction which erupted between the two groups. Quebec was divided into two colonies: Upper and Lower Canada. Upper Canada was British and Protestant, Lower Canada was French and Catholic.

The fur trade in Canada was dominated by two wealthy organizations, the North West Company and the Hudson's Bay Company. Both companies

SCOTT BRODIE

The placid beauty of Algonquin Park in northern Ontario.

Canada

The beautiful waterside city of Vancouver.

British Columbia in 1871, Prince Edward Island in 1873 and Alberta and Saskatchewan in 1905. Newfoundland opted to remain a separate British dominion until 1949, despite its precarious economic situation.

The confederation further enhanced Canada's popularity with migrants from Britain. The economy was bolstered by the opening of the western plains to wheat cultivation. Gold was discovered in the Klondike region of the frozen north in 1897. The subsequent

wielded immense power in the regions they occupied. Their rivalry was such that they went to war against each other. The dispute ended when the two were merged in 1821.

Canada became a popular destination for British immigrants during the first half of the nineteenth century. Fishing, fur trapping and agriculture dominated the economy. With prosperity came improved conditions in cities and towns. This, in turn, led to calls for greater political involvement. Britain, in an effort to prevent a revolution similar to that of the American colonies, granted internal self-government in 1848.

By this time the Britain's Canadian colonies were Nova Scotia, New Brunswick, New-foundland, Ontario (Upper Canada), Quebec (Lower Canada), British Columbia, Saskatchewan, Alberta and Prince Edward Island. The lands owned by the Hudsons Bay Company became Manitoba in 1870.

During the 1860s there were various conferences aimed at establishing a single political union of the colonies. The British North America Act of 1867 became the constitution of the Dominion of Canada. This new confederation included Ontario, New Brunswick, Nova Scotia and Quebec. Manitoba joined in 1870, followed by

A dam created by beavers in rural Canada.

The spectacular sweep of Niagara Falls on the Canada–USA border.

frantic gold rush was an enormous boost to Canadian finances. National unity came in the form of the transcontinental railway in 1885. This massive engineering achievement linked the country from east to west.

Friction between British and French cultures remained a very real problem. French Canadians resented Britain control of the confederation's foreign relations. They also opposed the involvement of Canadian troops in Britain's South African (Boer) War at the end of the nineteenth century.

Similarly, during World War I, Canadians fought with British forces in Europe. These troops were all volunteers prior to 1917. When the military draft was introduced, most French-Canadians refused to serve. A British-dominated coalition won power in 1917. Its policy was for mandatory military service regardless of cultural background.

Canada and some other British dominions began demanding a more independent voice in foreign relations in the 1920s. The Statute of Westminster was passed by the British parliament in 1931. This removed most of Britain's powers to control Canadian affairs.

Canada was a substantial participant in World War II from 1939. Its troops fought in areas from Hong Kong to Europe. They were part of the force which landed on the French coast on D-Day, June 6, 1944.

A new industrial capacity was created during the war. Canada embarked on a period of prosperity in the 1950s. A 1964 movement promoted a stronger national identity separate from Britain. The Canadian flag had Britain's Union Flag in the top left corner.

Despite some bitter opposition, the parliament eventually approved a new flag in 1965. Its two red stripes and stylized maple leaf design made it one of the most distinctive flags in the world.

The British–French divide had become more dramatic by the 1960s. Violence was threatening to shatter Canadian unity. The government of Prime Minister Pierre Trudeau introduced the policy of bilingualism in all government dealings. This failed to quell the province of Quebec's continued threats of

Canada

secession from the confederation. In 1980, the people of Quebec were granted a vote on whether to remain within Canada or leave. The bitter battle ended with a vote to remain.

The original British North America Act of 1867 did not allow Canadians to alter their own constitution. Trudeau began a series of debates which led to the British parliament passing the Canada Act in 1982. Canada became a wholly independent nation and adopted a new constitution.

Quebec refused to recognize the new constitution because it did not protect the status of French-Canadians. In an effort to solve the problem, conservative Prime Minister Brian Mulroney began negotiating the

Meech Lake Accord in 1987. The agreement failed after being rejected in a 1990 vote.

Canada, the United States and Mexico signed the North American Free Trade Agreement (NAFTA) in 1988. This resolution called for the elimination of trade barriers among the nations.

In 1991 Quebec again demanded greater constitutional powers, threatening to secede from the confederation. A complex set of constitutional amendments was designed to appease Quebec. Unfortunately, the amendments were rejected by voters. The Separatist movement's activities remain a major problem for the Canadian government. In 1995 the people of Quebec voted by

a thin margin to remain part of Canada.

The new Canadian constitution laid the groundwork for returning lands taken from indigenous people during colonial times. Vast tracts of land have been given back to the original inhabitants.

In 1999, Canada moved for reconciliation with the Inuit people of the northwest. Their own territory, called Nunavut, was carved out of the North West Territories. The Canadian government issued a formal apology to the native peoples for 150 years of mistreatment.

The lakeside buildings of Toronto.

Cape Verde

REPUBLIC OF CAPE VERDE

GOVERNMENT
Website www.governo.cv
Capital Praia
Type of government Republic
Independence from Portugal
July 5, 1975
Voting Universal adult suffrage
Head of state President
Head of government Prime
Minister
Constitution 1980, revised 1992,
1995, 1999
Legislature
Unicameral National Assembly
Judiciary Supreme Tribunal of
Justice
Member of IMF, OAU, UN,
UNESCO, WHO

LAND AND PEOPLE
Land area
1,557 sq mi (4033 sq km)
Highest point
Mount Pico do Cano
9,165 ft (2829 m)
Coastline 601 mi (965 km)
Population 408,760
Major cities and populations
Praia 95,000
Mindelo 63,000
Ethnic groups African-European
70%, African 30%
Religion Christianity
Languages
Portuguese (official)

ECONOMIC
Currency Cape Verdean escudo
Industry
food, beverages, fish processing,
footwear, garments, mining,
ship repair
Agriculture
bananas, corn, beans, sweet
potatoes, sugar cane, coffee,
peanuts, coconut, melons, livestock
Natural resources
salt, basalt rock, limestone,
kaolin, seafood

Cape Verde is a group of ten islands and five small islets in the Atlantic Ocean. It is located approximately 300 miles (480 km) west of Senegal, a country in western Africa. The land is arid and infertile, with the exception of a few valleys. Most of the mountainous landscape was formed as volcanoes. The weather is generally warm. Unreliable rainfall commonly causes serious drought.

Seventy percent of the population is of mixed African and European descent, while most of the others are African. Cape Verde is almost entirely Christian. Portuguese, the official language, is widely mixed with African languages to create a distinctive Criolo tongue.

The Cape Verde islands were uninhabited until European colonization. They were discovered by Portuguese navigators in 1456. A Portuguese settlement was established on Santiago six years later. Within a short time it had become central to the slave trade. Cape Verde was a major trans-shipment point for African slaves being sent to the Caribbean or Brazil. It was also a penal colony for Portuguese convicts. When the slave trade was abolished in 1876, activity on the islands decreased a good deal.

An armed struggle for the independence of Cape Verde and Portuguese Guinea began in 1961. The latter became Guinea-Bissau in 1973. Following the military coup d'état in Portugal in 1974, Cape Verde was placed under a transitional administration. Independence was declared on July 5, 1975. Aristides Pereira became the first president. Government since that time has been relatively stable.

The economy of Cape Verde is much affected by droughts which harm its meager farming industry. The nation is largely dependent upon aid from other countries. Focus is being placed on attracting foreign investors who might aid in varying the country's sources of revenue.

Fort Real do Sao Felipe.

LONELY PLANET IMAGES

Central African Republic

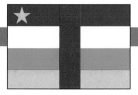

Landlocked Central African Republic is in the heart of Africa, close to the equator. Most of the land is a plateau with an average elevation of 2300 feet (700 m) covered by grasslands. The eastern areas are largely desert, while much of the south is dense forest. The climate is equatorial. Average warm temperatures vary little throughout the year.

Of the Republic's eighty ethnic groupings, the largest is the Baya. Others include the Banda, Sara, Mandija, and Mbdum. About half of the people are Christian, while most of the others practice indigenous beliefs. Sanga is the spoken language. French is used for writing. The Republic is a very poor nation with low rates of literacy and life expentancy.

The Baya and Banda peoples migrated to the area during the nineteenth century to escape slave traders in the nearby Congo Basin. The area became the French colony of Ubangi-Shari in 1898. It was incorporated into French Equatorial Africa in 1910. French companies were given land, which was developed by natives working as slaves.

Renamed the Central African Republic, it achieved independence within the French Community in 1958. Full independence followed on August 13, 1960, under President David Dacko.

Dacko was overthrown by Colonel Jean Bedel Bokassa in 1966. He nullified the constitution and took full executive control. A bizarre and brutal dictator, he crowned himself emperor in 1977. Foreign investment flowed in, particularly from France. It was reported that Bokassa ordered the massacre of eighty children. He was overthrown by the military aided by former president Dacko.

Dacko was reelected in a controversial poll in March 1981. Six months later General André Kolingba deposed him. This dictatorship lasted twelve years until multi-party elections were held. Ange-Félix Patassé was elected president. Economic and ethnic problems continued.

The unpaid army staged three mutinies in 1996. The last was put down by French forces. Despite a government of national unity, troops again mutinied in June 1997. A French military occupation was replaced in 1999 by an all-African peacekeeping force.

Patassé was reelected in 1998 but former President Kolingba continued to conspire with the army against him. A May 2001 coup d'état failed.

GOVERNMENT
Website www.rca-gouv.net/etoile.html
Capital Bangui
Type of government Republic
Independence from France August 13, 1960
Voting Universal adult suffrage
Head of state President
Head of government Prime Minister
Constitution 1995
Legislature Unicameral National Assembly
Judiciary Supreme Court
Member of IMF, OAU, UN, UNESCO, WHO, WTO

LAND AND PEOPLE
Land area 240,535 sq mi (622,984 sq km)
Highest point Mt. Gaou 4,600 ft (1420 m)
Population 3,642,739
Major cities and populations
Bangui 567,000
Bangassou 317,000
Ethnic groups
Baya 35%, Banda 30% Sara 10%, Mandija 9%, Mbdum 9%, others 7%
Religions Christianity 50%, Traditional animist 25%, Muslim 15%
Languages French (official), Sanga

ECONOMIC
Currency CFA franc
Industry
mining, timber milling, brewing, textiles, footwear, bicycle assembly
Agriculture
cotton, coffee, tapioca, yams, millet, corn, bananas; timber
Natural resources
bauxite, coal, copper, iron ore, tin, silver, uranium, nickel, tungsten, lead, zinc, diamonds, natural gas, petroleum

Chad

REPUBLIC OF CHAD

GOVERNMENT
Capital N'djaména
Type of government Republic
Independence from France
August 11, 1960
Voting Universal adult suffrage
Head of state President
Head of government Prime
Minister
Constitution 1996
Legislature
Bicameral Parliament
National Assembly (lower house),
Senate (upper house)
Judiciary Supreme Court
Member of IMF, OAU, UN,
UNESCO, WHO, WTO

LAND AND PEOPLE
Land area
495,755 sq mi (1,284,000 sq km)
Highest point Emi Koussi
11,204 ft (3415 m)
Population 8,997,237
Major cities and populations
N'djaména 550,000
Moundou 290,000
Bongor 205,000
Ethnic groups Bagirmi, Sara &
Kreish 35%, Sudanic Arab 25%,
Tubu 8%, Mbum 7%, others 25%
Religions Islam 40%, Christianity
33%, traditional animism 27%
Languages
French, Arabic (both official)
Over 100 indigenous languages

ECONOMIC
Currency CFA franc
Industry
textiles, mining, meat packing,
brewing, soap,
Agriculture
cotton, sorghum, millet, peanuts,
rice, potatoes, tapioca, cattle, sheep,
goats
Natural resources
uranium, sodium carbonate, kaolin

Chad is a landlocked country in north-central Africa. The low-lying areas of the Lake Chad Basin are surrounded on three sides by mountains and plateaus. The northern half of the country lies within the Sahara Desert. The climate is consistently warm. Summer rains fall in the southern areas, but the north gets hardly any rain at all.

There are two hundred ethnic groups in Chad. Northerners are nomadic Arabs. Southerners belong to more settled African cultures. The Bagirmi, Sara and Kreish peoples dominate the south. Islam is the religion of the northerners. Most people in the south follow traditional animist beliefs. Chad's people speak more than 100 different languages.

Western Chad was controlled by the Arab Kanem Empire from the ninth century A.D. This empire fell to Bornu in the sixteenth century. Various kingdoms to the south took control at intervals during the next centuries. The economy of the region became dependent upon the slave trade.

Rabah Zubayr from Sudan completed his conquest of Chad in the late nineteenth century. French armed forces seized control of the region from Zobeir soon afterward. Chad became part of French Equatorial Africa in 1910. The French did not upset the indigenous way of life. They established cotton growing plantations in the south. Chad became a separate colony in 1920.

Full independence came on August 11, 1960. President Francois Tombalbaye worked to end the economic domination of the slave traders. He was supported by the Bantu-speaking peoples of the south. A rebellion took place in 1966 led by northern Muslims with help from Libya. The French military suppressed the rebels.

Tombalbaye's assassination in 1975 sparked a leadership struggle between the military and civilians. A northerner, Goukouni Oueddei, became president in 1980. Libya intervened to provide protection from rebels led by Hissene Habre. Oueddi was deposed in 1982 and Habre, aided by French troops, became president. Libya was immediately expelled from Chad.

Further turmoil erupted in 1990 when Idriss Déby overthrew the government. Promised reforms were delayed and attempts at peace agreements failed. Clashes continued between rebels and the government troops. Déby was elected president in 1996, amid charges of election fraud surrounding both the presidential and legislative ballots. Déby was reelected in 2001.

Chile

BRAND X PICTURES

The beach at Valparaiso.

Chile stretches from north to south in a long narrow strip down the western coast of South America. The coastal plateau is backed by a cordillera, or mountain range, called the Andes. This runs the length of the country and provides a border with Argentina. In the far south the land culminates in a chain of spectacular fjords. Fjords are long, narrow sea inlets between steep cliffs. Although it is 2,650 miles (4,270 km) long, Chile has an average width of only 110 miles (180 km). Chile has been subject to numerous volcanoes and earthquakes.

Due to its varied geography, Chile has a wide variety of climatic conditions. The deserts of the north have little rainfall and relatively high temperatures. The center of the country, where most of the country's farm are located, is warm and rainy. The southern region varies from cool and rainy to very cold with violent storms from the ocean.

Eighty-five percent of Chileans live in cities. Ninety percent are mestizos, people with mixed Spanish and indigenous heritage. There are also mestizos with British, Irish, Italian, Yugoslav and German ancestry. The only large indigenous group of any size is the Mapuche. These people live in the eastern border regions. Some ninety percent of the population is Christian and Spanish is the official language.

Mining is a key part of Chile's economy. It is the world's largest copper producer, Iron ore and manganese are also important minerals. The agricultural industry produces only fifty percent of the country's needs. The main crops are wheat, beans, beet sugar, corn, potatoes and fruit. Chile has recently become a prominent wine exporter. Sheep, grown for both wool and meat, are the dominant livestock. Principal manufactured goods include processed foods, textiles, cement, machinery, timber products, iron and steel, paper and chemicals.

Chile's constitution came into effect in 1981 and was amended eight years later. The people elect the president directly for a six-year term. There is a cabinet with twenty ministers appointed by the president. The legislature is bicameral, with a partly elected and partly appointed Senate. The Chamber of Deputies, the lower house, is wholly elected. Chile's thirteen regions control local government.

Until the sixteenth century, what is now Chile was split into two distinct regions. The north was part of the Inca empire, the south was controlled by the Araucanians. In 1535, the Spanish conquistador Francisco Pizarro sent Diego de Almagro to establish a settlement in the south. Crossing the Andes from

Peru, he met powerful resistance from the Araucanians who repelled the invasion. Pedro de Valdivia was more successful four years later, despite further fierce resistance. A Spanish settlement was established at Santiago in 1541. Chile was a part of the Peru viceroyalty until 1778.

The Araucanians maintained a bitter and bloody war against the Spanish into the nineteenth century. Having little apparent mineral wealth, Chile was developed as an agricultural settlement. As resistance declined, settlers established large estates, using the indigenous peoples as laborers.

As was true of other Spanish possessions, Chile saw its chance for independence in

1810 when Spain was under the control of France. The movement was led by Bernardo O'Higgins. Rebels deposed the colonial government. Spanish troops appeared from Peru and reinstated the government in 1814.

During 1818, Independence leader José de San Martin marched an army across the Andes from Argentina in very difficult conditions. His perseverance was rewarded by victory at the battle of Maipú at which Spanish forces were overcome. The last royalists were defeated in 1826.

Bernardo O'Higgins became leader of an independent Chile on February 12, 1818, with the title of supreme director. The military, assisted by a group of intellectuals, created an autocratic government which lasted fifteen years.

O'Higgins was forced to resign in 1823. He was replaced by a succession of liberal-minded leaders. Friction between those leading the movement for democracy and land-owning families erupted into a civil war between 1829 and 1831.

When peace came, the new president, Joaquin Prieto, began a process of reform which led to a new constitution in 1833. War hero President Manuel Bulnes led a conserva-

Snow-capped Mount Osorma.

GOVERNMENT
Website www.presidencia.cl
Capital Santiago
Type of government Republic
Independence from Spain
September 18, 1810
Voting
Universal adult suffrage, compulsory
Head of state President
Head of government President
Constitution 1981,
amended 1989, 1993, 1997
Legislature
Bicameral National Congress
Chamber of Deputies (lower house),
Senate (upper house)
Judiciary Supreme Court
Member of APEC, IMF, OAS, UN,
UNESCO, WHO, WTO

LAND AND PEOPLE
Land area
292,134 sq mi (756,626 sq km)
Highest point
Ojos del Salado 22,572 ft (6880 m)
Coastline 4,010 mi (6435 km)
Population 15,498,930
Major cities and populations
Santiago 5,200,000
Concepción 355,000
Viña del Mar 290,000
Ethnic groups
Mestizos 92%,
Religions Christianity 99%
Languages
Spanish (official), indigenous
languages

ECONOMIC
Currency Chilean peso
Industry
mining, food processing, iron, steel,
wood products, transport equipment,
cement, textiles
Agriculture
wheat, corn, grapes, beans, beet
sugar, potatoes, fruit, beef, poultry,
wool, seafoods, timber
Natural resources
copper, timber, iron ore, nitrates,
precious metals, molybdenum

Chile

BRAND X PICTURES

tive government from 1841 to 1851. He formalized the separation of the country's executive, legislative and judicial powers. A new economic policy promoted the export of minerals and the import of finished goods. Duties and tariffs on imported goods financed considerable social development.

As Chile's borders had never been accurately defined, there were numerous disputes with neighbors. Chile's seizure of the Atacama nitrate deposits from Bolivia and Peru led to the 1879 War of the Pacific. After victory in 1883, Chile began making vast profits from the mines. Chile was industrializing rapidly by the twentieth century. Its economy became one of the most successful in South America.

The parliamentary republic established in 1891 was notorious for its corruption. When the military staged a coup d'état in 1924, one of their first actions was to impose strict controls on labor unions. Colonel Carlos Ibañez was elected president in 1927. He resigned four years later when Chile's economy collapsed during the Depression.

Economic turmoil prompted a rapid turn to the left in Chilean politics. The socialist-communist Popular Front came to power in 1938. President Pedro Cerda exerted considerable control over the economy. After initially siding with Germany in World War II, Chile changed sides in 1943. President Gabriel González Videla, under pressure from the United States, banned the Communist Party from Chile in 1948.

Chile was racked by labor disputes and climbing inflation through the 1950s and 1960s. Eduardo Frei Montalva was elected president in 1964. He began a program of land reform and education. His government took a controlling interest in formerly American-owned copper mines.

Chileans elected Salvador Allende Gossens president in 1970. He led the Popular Unity Front, a coalition of left-leaning parties. Allende was the first president in a non-communist country to be elected on an openly Marxist-Leninist policy platform. Allende nationalized the copper industry and other mainly U.S.-owned corporations. He froze prices and boosted wages. The United States retaliated with a trade embargo. Then inflation soared.

Right-wing elements orchestrated a strike of business owners and professionals in 1972. Allende was pressured to appoint several members of the military to his cabinet. The military, backed by the United States, staged a bloody coup in 1973. Allende was assassinated and thousands of his supporters were murdered, deported or imprisoned.

General Augusto Pinochet Ugarte was then appointed president of Chile. His attempts to privatize state-owned enterprises did little to curb the economy's slide downward. All communist and socialist groups were made illegal in 1973, in hopes of ending public dissent. Four years later all other political parties were banned. Human rights abuses by the Pinochet regime drew the world's attention.

A new constitution in 1981 guaranteed elections by 1989. Slowly but surely, as Chile's economy deteriorated further, new opposition groups formed. The Catholic Church harshly criticized Pinochet. His attempt to remain president until 1997 was thwarted in a 1988 vote.

Christian Democrat Patricio Aylwin Azócar was elected president in 1989. His economic reforms were helpful, but the military strongly opposed his human rights initiatives. In 1990, as an act of reconciliation, Allende's remains were interred next to other former Chilean presidents. Aylwin pressed forward with reforms, while constantly working to appease the Pinochet-led military. He wanted to prevent another coup. His government made impressive advances in reducing inflation and poverty.

Eduardo Frei Ruiz-Tagle became president in 1994. His economic reforms brought countless new foreign investment to the country. The next president, elected in January 2000, was Ricardo Lagos Escobar, the first socialist since Allende. He is a moderate leader, intent on continuing to stabilize both Chile's economy and its fragile democracy.

In 1998, on a visit to Britain, Pinochet was arrested on a warrant for his extradition to Spain. Following a long period of legal discussion, he was released and allowed to return to Chile due to ill-health.

The stark coastline of Antofagasta la Portada.

BRAND X PICTURES

China

FLAT EARTH PICTURE GALLERY

The memorial to Mao Zedong in Tiananmen Square, Beijing.

China dominates eastern Asia. Its long coastline faces the Pacific Ocean, the East China Sea, and the South China Sea. There are rugged mountains in nearly half of the country. Much of north and north central China is mountainous desert. In the northeast, the Manchurian and North China plains feature fertile farmlands. The eastern areas are predominantly low-lying. They are crossed by the vast Yangtze and Huang He rivers. To the west of these is the Loess Plateau. In the far southwest, lies the Tibetan Plateau. This plateau is the world's highest.

Covering such a vast distance from north to south means China's climatic range is huge. The climate is very much influenced by monsoon winds from the oceans. Northern winters bring bitter cold as dry winds blow in from Siberia. Southern regions are hot and humid much of the year. Hong Kong can be quite cold. Central China experiences a short, cold winter and suffers furnace-like heat in summer. The areas nearest the oceans usually receive a good deal of rainfall. Southern coastal regions are subject to damaging typhoons.

Eighty percent of China's people live in Manchuria, a region in northeast China. Most of them are of Han Chinese origin. Others include a

wide range of ethnic minorities including the Zhuang, Hui, Manchu, Uigur, and Yi.

The government discourages all religion. Buddhism and Taoism are both strong. However, the Buddhist-based Falun Gong movement has been strongly-suppressed by the government. There are about seven million Christians and a small Muslim minority.

Mandarin Chinese is the official language, although many dialects are spoken, especially in the south. Cantonese is widely spoken in Hong Kong. Other southern dialects include Hakka and Wu. Written Chinese is universal. Most people use a simplified version of writing developed in the 1960s.

More than fifty percent of China's population is involved in agriculture. For many years, all agricultural activity was conducted through a collective system. Community members worked as a group to cultivate the land. The economic reforms of the 1980s swept this away, enabling individuals to control their own plots of land. The result was a substantial increase in agricultural yields.

China is the world's largest producer of rice and wheat, mainly for domestic consumption. Livestock farming is concentrated in the northern and western regions. Much agriculture continues to be very labor intensive. Farmers often use manual methods instead of modern machines.

Exploitation of mineral wealth forms a substantial part of China's economy. High-quality coal, found in abundance in the north and northeast, is used to generate electricity and provide power for older industries. Ample oil reserves lie off China's coastline. Since World War II, the nation's petroleum industry has grown immensely. At the end of the twentieth century, China was the world's fifth-largest oil producer and a major exporter.

In the communist heyday of the 1950s and 1960s, vast industrial plants produced all kinds of products. Since then Chinese industry has undergone a major transformation. Today the major growth comes from smaller factories producing consumer goods or high-technology products.

Special Economic Zones were established during the 1980s, primarily in southern China. In these regions, foreign investors were allowed to establish manufacturing facilities without the usual Communist controls. Efficient factories began producing good for export from Hong Kong. The Special Economic Zones have become the wealthiest parts of China.

Despite all the changes of recent years, China remains firmly under the control of the

GOVERNMENT
Website www.gov.cn
Capital Beijing
Type of government Communist state
Voting Universal adult suffrage
Head of state President
Head of government Premier
Constitution 1982
Legislature Unicameral National People's Congress (Quanguo Renmin Daibiao Dahui)
Judiciary Supreme People's Court
Member of APEC, IMF, UN, UNESCO, UNHCR, WHO, WTO

LAND AND PEOPLE
Land area 3,696,100 sq mi (9,572,900 sq km)
Highest point Mount Everest 28,674 ft (8,850 m)
Coastline 9040 mi (14,550 km)
Population 1,284,303,705
Major cities and populations
Shanghai 12 million
Beijing 9 million
Tianjin 8 million
Shenyang 6 million
Hong Kong 6 million
Guangzhou 4.1 million
Ethnic groups Han Chinese 92%, various minorities 8%
Religions Buddhism, Taoism, Christianity, Islam practiced
Languages Mandarin Chinese, with numerous dialects

ECONOMIC
Currency Yuan
Industry
mining, machinery, textiles, clothing, petroleum, cement, fertilizers, footwear, food processing, motor vehicles, electronics
Agriculture
rice, wheat, potatoes, sorghum, peanuts, tea, millet, barley, cotton, oil pork
Natural resources
coal, oil, iron ore, petroleum, natural gas, mercury, tin, tungsten, antimony, manganese, vanadium, magnetite, aluminum, lead, zinc, uranium

China

senior members of the Communist Party. The nation's constitution has evolved from the original adopted in 1949. There is a unicameral legislature, known as the National People's Congress (NPC). Its members, called deputies, are elected for five-year terms. The NPC is responsible for overall economic strategy and is able to amend the constitution. However, the NPC never acts without authorisation from the leadership of the Communist Party.

Archeologists have determined that early Chinese peoples lived around 5000 B. C. in the area of the Huang He (Yellow) River around 5000 B.C. These groups worked as farmers, made pottery, and worshipped gods in nature.

The first records of Chinese history are from about 1750 B.C. when the Shang dynasty was established. The Shang occupied part of northern central China. They grew a large variety of crops and raised livestock as well as silkworms. Shang artisans are credited with making high quality bronze artifacts, utensils and weapons.

The Shang created a highly class-conscious society. The emperor and his nobles were at the top. Artisans, priests and warriors were the middle class, while the farmers and slaves were the lowest group.

At around 1100 B.C., the Shang dynasty was overthrown by the Chou dynasty. Land was divided up among various nobles, creating a feudal regime. Over the next 750 years Chou produced a number of philosophers, the most prominent being Gong Fuzi (Confucius) and Lao Tzu. The foundations of Chinese culture and ethics developed during this time.

In 221 B.C., the king of Ch'in declared himself First Emperor began the Ch'in dynasty. He reunited the entire country, creating forty-two provinces, each with a civil governor. He built a new capital near present-day Xi'an, requiring all nobles to live there, away from their supporters and armies. The imperial army was the only military body permitted, ir an effort to prevent uprisings against the emperor.

The First Emperor pressed men into military service to conquer other lands. He forced others to build the first Great Wall and many grand public structures. In an effort to control people's thoughts, he burned books. The First Emperor died after one of numerous rebellions.

The death of the emperor plunged China into civil war from which two leaders emerged. Xiang Hu declared himself emperor of Chu, and Liu Bang was proclaimed emperor of Han. After four years of conflict Xiang Hu committed suicide. Liu Bang founded the Han dynasty in 206 B.C.

ELECTRA COLLECTION

British and French warehouses at Guangzhou in the nineteenth century.

A prosperous southern Chinese merchant in the nineteenth century.

The new emperor wanted to build on the many strengths developed under the Ch'in dynasty. He lowered taxes and adopted a more humane treatment of the people. He established Confucianism as the official religion of the country.

A merit system for hiring government workers by the Han. Men wishing to enter the civil service were given a test. Schools opened across the empire to fulfill the new need for knowledge. People came to believe that learning would provide power and prosperity.

During the next 400 years of relative peace, some fine artistic traditions were established. Chinese explorers traveled to the Caspian Sea region and northern India. They returned with horses, which greatly enhanced China's military power. A trade route, known as the Silk Road, soon developed between East and West.

Apart from trade, the new routes to the West brought missionaries. Indian traders introduced Buddhism, which was adopted enthusiastically by many Chinese. Buddhism presented a serious challenge to Confucianism.

When the Han dynasty collapsed the empire split into three warring factions: Wei, Shu and Wu. The Wei emerged victorious and the Western T'sin, or Chin dynasty, was established in A.D. 265. It lasted until 317, when a period of turmoil began. During the Chin dynasty, the north and south had been reunited. For more than a century to follow they were again under separate rule.

In 589 General Yang Chien reunited China under his Sui dynasty. It lasted until 618 before collapsing under the weight of its corruption and rebellions. Li Yuan, a nobleman, led a force that captured Chang'an. He founded the Tang dynasty, which remained in place from 618 to 906.

The territory of China was expanded to its greatest extent under rulers of the Tang dynasty. Central government was reinstated and, for the first time, a standard language brought unity to the vastness of China. Confucianism once more became the guiding philosophy.

Tang's collapse in 907 led to a period known as the Five Dynasties, which lasted fifty years. Various military leaders established separate empires during this time.

Chaos reigned until 960 when the Sung dynasty was founded, ushering in a new period of progress and artistic development. During this time, printing processes greatly improved with the introduction of movable type. The development of gunpowder greatly changed methods of warfare.

The Sung dynasty lasted until 1279. For many years China was under almost constant siege by the Mongol armies of Genghis Khan. Eventually all of China fell to Mongol control, led by Genghis Khan's grandson Kublai. Thus began the legendary Yuan dynasty.

Kublai Khan launched a program of major public works, constructing networks of canals and roads. Despite efforts to win over his Chinese subjects,

China

FLAT EARTH PICTURE GALLERY

A worker in rural China.

he had to rely on Mongol and Turkish administrators to keep the empire under control. Kublai Khan converted to Buddhism and made Beijing his capital city. He encouraged trade and commerce, which was simplified with a standard system of currency. Explorer Marco Polo arrived from Europe during his reign.

After Kublai Khan's death in 1294, the Yuan dynasty declined rapidly. A number of Mongol successors ruled until 1368, when a former Buddhist monk named Chu Yuanzhang led an army that drove the Mongols from Beijing. The Ming dynasty, which he established, was ruled by ideas similar to those of the Sung dynasty.

The 1,500 acre (600 ha) Imperial City was completed at Beijing in the early fifteenth century. Within its boundaries was the Forbidden City, into which only the emperor, his family and staff could enter. The Great Wall of China was enlarged and fortified with masonry.

China was confronted in the sixteenth century by Portuguese mariners demanding trading rights. After numerous confrontations, China granted to Portugal an area in southern China called Macau. Here the Portuguese established communities and soon discovered good profits could be made by importing opium from India.

The Portuguese were followed by the Spanish. In 1604, the Dutch gained trading rights with little difficulty because they agreed to pay tribute to the Ming emperor.

The end of the Ming dynasty in 1644 was brought about by the Manchu people, who created the Ch'ing dynasty. Like the Mongols, the Manchus ruled China by military force. The Manchus managed to put down rebellions and to bring peace and prosperity to China.

In 1757, Emperor Ch'ien Lung blocked the access of European traders to all Chinese

ports other than Guangzhou. Barter trading was terminated, with the ruling that all goods had to be paid for in silver. When the British East India Company discovered Chinese merchants would accept opium in place of silver, trade resumed. Abundant opium grew in British-held Bengal.

There were tens of thousands of opium addicts in China by 1839. The emperor ordered his armies to seize the stocks of opium from the traders in Guangzhou, provoking what became known as the Opium Wars. In 1840, a British naval force arrived off Guangzhou, escorting ships loaded with opium as payment for the season's crop of tea. In

Macao's elegant Portuguese-influenced architecture.

SCOTT BRODIE

huge demand in England, tea was grown only in China.

After a number of sea battles, British troops landed and made their way inland. Shanghai had been captured and Nanjing was set to fal by June of 1842. The defeated Chinese signed the Treaty of Nanjing in August. Among the provisions, Hong Kong was ceded to Britain, and Guangzhou, Fuzhou, Xiamen, Ningbo and Shanghai were opened to trade.

The Second Opium War occurred in 1856–57. A minor incident on the Pearl River sparked an assault on the Chinese government by British forces. This led to the Treaties of Tianjin, which opened up more ports to foreign trade and allowed Christian missionaries to work anywhere in China.

The Ch'ing dynasty had been weakened by decades of internal unrest. The disastrous Opium Wars made things worse. One outcome was the Taiping Rebellion of 1851, led by Hung Hsiu-QCh-uan, who planned to convert China to Christianity. The rebels had established their capital at Nanjing within two years. The Europeans forced further concessions from the emperor in exchange for military assistance. Then the foreigners helped the Chinese to destroy the Taiping rebels.

The grand sweep of the Great Wall of China.

In the latter part of the 1800s, Western powers and Japan wanted to limit China's power in Southeast Asia. The Japanese invaded Korea in 1894, driving out the Chinese. Korea was given its independence. China also surrendered Formosa (now Taiwan) and the Liaodong Peninsula to Japan.

China came under the control of Dowager Empress Hz'u Hsi in the late 1800s. She exercised power briefly before passing it to her nephew Kuang Hsu.

FLAT EARTH PICTURE GALLERY

China

Although closely controlled by his aunt, Kuang Hsu was influenced by foreigners who wished to modernize China. He established a university and many schools in 1898. Manufacturing was encouraged, a banking system was introduced and free speech was permitted.

Tz'u Hsi wanted none of this reform. She had the emperor arrested and resumed control herself. In 1900, she orchestrated the Boxer Rebellion, staged by members of a secret society dedicated to evicting foreigners from China.

They massacred Christian missionaries and their converts before laying siege to the European interests in Beijing. The Japanese and German ambassadors were assassinated. The foreigners withstood the siege for fifty-five days before reinforcements arrived and repelled the Boxers.

Tz'u Hsi, having fled Beijing, returned in 1902, proposing a major program of modernization and a new constitutional government. In the meantime, a reform movement led by Sun Yat-Sen had gained considerable power. The revolution had spread across the nation by 1911. Sun Yat-Sen was made provisional president of a Chinese republic. China's imperial system had ended with the fall of the Manchu dynasty.

Sun Yat-Sen resigned a year later in favor of Yuan Shih-K'ai, believing only this military leader could unite all of China. Yuan Shih-Kai's government was marked by authoritarianism and brutality, provoking a number of unsuccessful revolts.

When the Kuomintang (KMT) — National People's Party — was formed in 1912, Sun Yat Sen pledged his support. The following year it won a majority of seats in the National Assembly. Yuan Shih Kai, fearing Sun's influence, expelled KMT members from

Part of the spectacular high-rise architecture of Hong Kong.

Water buffalo are commonly used for agricultural work in China.

the assembly and declared himself dictator.

Japan, seeing an opportunity to expand its control, landed troops in Germany's Shandong territory in 1914. Yuan was forced to accept a list of demands from Japan. Following World War I, Japan was awarded Shandong province by the Versailles Conference.

Yuan declared himself emperorin 1915. Provincial governors rebelled against his rule. China became unstable when he died a year later. Warlords who controlled various parts of the country now saw an opportunity to increase their power and wealth.

Twelve men met secretly in Shanghai to form the Communist Party of China in 1921. Supported by the Soviet Union (USSR), they planned to infiltrate trade unions and worker groups. Sun Yat-Sen, heeding advice from the Soviets, reorganized the Kuomintang. Communists would be included in the new KMT membership.

Following Sun's death in 1925, KMT leadership passed to Chiang Kai-Shek. He led a military expedition to reunify China, ridding it of the warlords. By 1928, the mission of the Kuomintang under Chiang Kai-Shek was moderately successful.

Next Chiang Kai-Shek turned on his Communist allies. Many of the leaders were executed and Communist-allied trade groups were targeted. After widespread bloodletting the Communists, led by Mao Zedong, fled to a remote mountain hideout. Here they organized a peasant army.

Chiang went after them with great determination. By 1934 the Communists found themselves losing the battle. Mao Zedong and 100,000 supporters embarked on what became known as the Long March. For a year they faced pressures from the Nationalists as well as China's difficult climate and geography. Only 7,000 arrived in Shaanxi province at the end of the 6,000 mile (9,500 km) march.

With Chiang battling the Communists, Japan took the opportunity to invade Manchuria in 1931. From this base they moved south. While Chiang preferred to defeat the Communists first, many Nationalists disagreed. They staged the Xi'an Incident in December of 1936. Chiang was kidnapped in an effort to force him into an alliance with the Communists against the Japanese.

The Communists agreed to work with the Nationalists. However, the far better disciplined Communist army was much more effective than Chi-

ang's corruption-ridden forces. The Communists took the opportunity to liberate millions of peasants, winning them over to the cause. Communism's image was also aided by the brutality displayed by the Japanese invaders.

When Japan declared war against the Western Allies in 1941, China received considerable military support from the United States. The shaky Communist–Nationalist truce fell apart once World War II ended.

The Soviet Union occupied Manchuria after Japan's sur-

Sun Yat Sen and his wife Choong Ching Ling.

ELECTRA COLLECTION

China

Cooking for a street café.

render. When the time came for them to depart, they handed the territory to the Communists. From this base the Communists attacked the southern Nationalist-held regions. Shenyang fell to the Communists in November of 1948.

It became apparent that Chiang Kai Shek's forces, despite considerable U.S. support, were losing the struggle. Heavy-handed repression of the population, economic instability and famine tipped the balance in favor of Mao Zedong's Communists.

Communist forces won their greatest psychological victory in January of 1949 when Beijing fell with minimal fighting.

Other major cities followed during the rest of that year. Mao declared a Central Communist government on October 1, 1949, under the name of the People's Republic of China.

Nationalist forces crumbled as Communist control spread across China. Protected by the U.S. Navy's Seventh Fleet, Chiang Kai Shek and his remaining supporters fled to the island of Formosa (now Taiwan). A Nationalist government was established there in 1949.

While both the Communists and the Nationalists claimed to be the official government of China, the Communists occupied the large bulk of the country. Their government was legitimized by official recognition from Britain, India and other nations. The United States continued to maintain that Chiang's Taiwan-based regime was the legitimate ruling body of China.

The Communists moved quickly to consolidate their power and clean out the last pockets of Nationalist resistance. Many people fled China, pouring into the British enclave of Hong Kong. While some went on to other parts of the world, many stayed to create the economic powerhouse that Hong Kong became.

Mao and his followers launched a classic communist-style government. Economic intervention brought runaway

inflation under control and problems of food distribution were gradually sorted out.

Individual ownership of farms was abolished and a collective system introduced during the 1950s. All industry was nationalized and substantial aid flowed in from the Soviet Union. Industrialization was promoted to ensure independence from the non-communist world.

As part of the Communist conversion, government representatives were sent to all parts of China. They conducted trials of those considered to be exploiters of the peasants. Most of these people were landlords, moneylenders, black marketeers. As many as two million of those tried were executed.

China became a major player in the Cold War in October 1950. On the Korean peninsula, United Nations forces had pushed the invading North Korean army out of the south and were pursuing it toward the Chinese border. The Chinese army swept across the Yalu River to defend the North. It drove General Douglas MacArthur's forces into retreat.

Mao launched the Great Leap Forward in 1958. His intent was to make China a world industrial power. He sought to increase agricultural production while reducing consumption. Extreme haste and bad planning led the program to fail.

Simultaneously, a much-reduced agricultural labor force could not plant and harvest sufficient crops. Between 1959 and 1961, widespread famine resulted. Millions of people died for lack of food during this time.

After its hard-line leader Joseph Stalin died in 1953, the Soviet Union improved its relations with the non-communist world, particularly western Europe. Relations between the two communist giants deteriorated due to China's opposition to such change.

By 1960, the Soviet Union had withdrawn all technical assistance to China and ceased aid payments. War between the two nations seemed likely. Soviet and Chinese armies faced each other across their long border in China's north. While minor battles were fought, a major confrontation never occurred.

China promoted communist movements in other parts of Asia, notably Indonesia, Malaysia and Thailand. Initially a supporter of the Vietnamese communists, the relationship soured when Vietnam moved closer to the Soviet Union. Support for China among non-communist Asian nations soon evaporated when Chinese-sup-

A mural celebrating the success of the communist revolution.

China

ported groups attempted to overthrow their governments.

Military interventions gradually gave way to diplomatic measures. The Chinese became competitors with the Soviet Union, promoting communism in impoverished nations. Chinese technical advisers were a common sight in poor Asian and African nations in the 1960s and 1970s.

By the mid-1960s dissension appeared within the Communist Party as various factions jockeyed for power. Mao's status had been damaged by the failure of the Great Leap Forward. He launched the Cultural Revolution in 1966 in an effort to regain his stature.

Fanatical young Mao supporters, known as Red Guards, were encouraged to bring the nation back to the pure ideals of the 1949 revolution. This was Mao's way of curbing any challenge to his leadership. The initiative did considerable damage as Red Guards scoured the nation searching for 'traitors'.

It was reported that Defense Minister Lin Biao died in an air crash in 1971. Supposedly he was fleeing to the Soviet Union after a failed attempt to assassinate Mao. It is more likely Lin was assassinated because he was close to overthrowing Mao as chairman.

Under pressure from the United States, the United Nations maintained Taiwan (the Republic of China) as the official representative of China in the General Assembly. Reality dawned in 1971 when Taiwan was expelled and the People's Republic replaced it.

The United States had proposed a 'two Chinas' policy, with both nations taking seats in the UN. China's growing strength as an economic and political power forced the U.S. to soften its attitudes. These changes were illustrated dramatically in February 1972, when President Richard Nixon visited Beijing.

By the 1970s, hard-line Chinese communism was disappearing under the more liberal Deng Xiao Peng and Zhou En Lai. On the opposite side the Gang of Four, one of whom was Mao's wife, pushed the pure communist ideology. Mao, still the great figurehead, was torn between the moderates and the Gang of Four.

When Zhou died, the Gang of Four convinced an aging Mao that Deng's modernization compromised Mao's revolution-

FLAT EARTH PICTURE GALLERY

A street scene in Beijing

FLAT EARTH PICTURE GALLERY

Chinese children on a school outing.

ary ideals. Deng was removed from leadership in 1976 and replaced by Hua Guo Feng. After Mao's death in September the liberals convinced Hua to have the Gang of Four charged and arrested.

Deng returned to power in 1977 as deputy chairman. In reality, he was the most powerful man in China. A major modernization plan created a favorable atmosphere for foreign companies to invest in China. The collective farms system ended, leading to healthy increases in agricultural production. Special Economic Zones were created in which foreign companies could establish factories.

In 1984 British Prime Minister Margaret Thatcher responded to Chinese pressure for the return of Hong Kong to China. The dynamic city was returned in 1997 when the 99-year lease on the New Territories expired. Similarly, negotiations with Portugal ended with an agreement for Macau to become part of China once again in 1999.

In 1989 General Secretary Hu Yao Bang was removed from office by conservatives who opposed his views on personal freedoms. He was replaced by Zhao Ziyang. When Hu died in 1989, student memorials turned into protests in Beijing's Tiananmen Square.

Having tolerated demands for democratic reform for a long time, the government sent in troops who violently broke up the gatherings. Hundreds died and many more were arrested, sparking international outrage. Subsequent economic sanctions had a dramatic effect on China's economy. Despite efforts to regain international support, its relations with many countries is strained.

In the early 1990s, upon the release of its dissident prisoners, the United States resumed diplomatic relations with China. The People's Congress elected Jiang Zemin president in 1993. U. S. President Bill Clinton visited China in 1998, at which time he debated human right issues with Jiang Zemin. Relations between the U. S. and China weakened again in 1999 when a U. S. aircraft accidentally bombed the Chinese embassy in Belgrade, Yugoslavia, killing more than 20 Chinese diplomats.

Taiwan's status remains an international problem. The United States continues to pledge military support in the event of an invasion by China. Taiwan is now a major economic power. Most of its people do not want reintegration with the People's Republic of China. However, China still appears intent on regaining control of Taiwan.

Colombia

REPUBLIC OF COLOMBIA

Bogota, the capital of Colombia.

Located in the northwest of South America, Colombia lies immediately south of Central America. It is divided by three sections of the Colombian Andes mountain range. There are heavily forested lowlands in the Amazon basin. Wide coastal plains front the Caribbean Sea to the north and the Pacific Ocean in the west. The climate varies, but is generally tropical. The Amazon lowlands experience very heavy rainfall.

Most Colombians live in urban areas. Approximately sixty per cent are mestizo, of both European and indigenous descent. Twenty percent are of a mixed European-African heritage. Indigenous inhabitants account for only one percent of the population.

Almost everyone is Christian, mostly Catholic. Spanish is the official language, while close to 200 indigenous dialects are also spoken.

Coffee is Colombia's major export. Other crops include sugar cane, bananas, palm oil, cotton, potatoes, fruits and vegetables. Among Colombia's principal mineral resources are iron ore, nickel, gold, coal, copper, silver, platinum, emeralds, oil and natural gas. Manufacturing industries include cement, chemicals, processed foods, clothing and textiles.

At least a quarter of Colombia's foreign earnings comes from illegal narcotics. Some of the raw coca processed is homegrown, the rest brought in from Bolivia and Peru. The formerly large tourist industry has been affected by violence relatd to the drug trade.

Before colonization, Colombia was inhabited by the Chibcha people, who were farmers living in the northwestern mountains. Spain annexed the region to gain control of gold mines after 1525. The state of New Granada included Colombia, Ecuador, Venezuela and Panama.

Colombians rebelled against Spanish rule on July 20, 1810, in a popular uprising at Bogotá led by Antonio Nariño. Simón Bolívar's army achieved liberation at the Battle of Boyacà after a nine-year struggle.

The new state of Greater Colombia included Colombia, Ecuador, Venezuela and Panama, with Bolívar as president. Venezuela and Ecuador became separate nations in 1830. Colombia and Panama were called the Granadine Confederation from 1858 until 1863 when the union was renamed the United States of Colombia.

Colombia's government regularly shifted between liberal and conservative factions, often violently. The War of a Thousand Days erupted in 1899. By the end of this war in 1901, about 100,000 people had died.

The state of Panama separated from Colombia to facilitate the United States' construction of the Panama Canal in 1903. The arrangement caused strained relations between the U. S. and Colombia for almost two decades.

Enríque Herrera's election to the presidency in 1930 was Colombia's first peaceful change of power. Subsequently, Colombians enjoyed many economic and social advances. However, widespread riots occurred when liberal leader Jorge Eliécer Gaitán was assassinated in Bogotá in 1948.

The conservative Laureano Gómez took power in 1950. His dictatorship lasted until a military coup in 1953. Army leader Gustavo Rojas Pinilla replaced him, ushering in a period of repression and corruption. Another coup in 1957, backed by both factions, deposed Rojas Pinilla. Relative stability followed the 1958 elections.

The United States' demand for illegal narcotics greatly enriched Colombia's criminals, beginning in the late 1960s. Durg lords took control of politics and maintained powerful gangs to protect them.

The left-wing Revolutionary Armed Forces of Colombia (FARC) guerrillas came to prominence during this same time. They clashed with government forces and assassinated key officials. Liberal president César Gaviria Trujillo's 1991 constitution guaranteed human rights and social services. Nevertheless, during the 1990s drug cartels maintained a huge influence on Colombian life.

President Ernesto Samper Pizano, elected in 1994, was constantly accused of corruption. The United States, claiming that this president was the pawn of drug lords, refused further economic aid.

Conservative President Andrés Pastrana Arango, elected in 1998, turned to the United States for help in fighting the cocaine trade. The U. S. Congress approved a $1.3 billion aid package in 2000. These funds were intended for an improved military and the creation of incentive to farmers to grow crops other than coca.

Álvaro Uribe Vélez was sworn in as president on August 8, 2002. During the ceremony in Bogota, leftist guerrillas fired mortar rounds into the city, killing fourteen people. The president has vowed to strengthen both the police and the military to crack down on the drug trade.

GOVERNMENT
Website www.presidencia.gov.co
Capital Bogotá
Type of government Republic
Independence from Spain
July 20, 1810
Voting Universal adult suffrage
Head of state President
Head of government President
Constitution 1991
Legislature
Bicameral Congress
House of Representatives (lower house), Senate (upper house)
Judiciary Supreme Court
Member of IMF, OAS, UN, UNESCO, UNHCR, WHO, WTO

LAND AND PEOPLE
Land area 440,830 sq mi (1,141,748 sq km)
Highest point
Cristobal Colon 18,947 ft (5775 m)
Coastline 1,999 mi (3208 km)
Population 41,008,227
Major cities and populations
Bogotá 5.6 million
Cali 1.9 million
Medellin 1.9 million
Barranquilla 1.1 million
Ethnic groups
Mestizo 60%, European 20%, African-European 15%
Religions Christianity 97%, traditional beliefs 2%
Languages
Spanish, many indigenous languages

ECONOMIC
Currency Colombian peso
Industry textiles, food processing, oil, clothing, footwear, beverages, chemicals, cement, mining
Agriculture
coffee, cut flowers, bananas, rice, corn, sugar cane, cacao beans, oilseed, vegetables; forest products,
Natural resources
petroleum, natural gas, coal, iron ore, nickel, gold, copper, emeralds

Comoros

UNION OF COMOROS

The islands of the Comoros are located in the Mozambique Channel between eastern Africa and Madagascar. The islands were formed by volcanos. On Njazidja, the country's largest island, the nation's active volcano is also its highest peak. The island of Mwali is the most fertile, while Grand Comore and Nzwani have very poor farming terrain. The climate is tropical with great heat and humidity between November and April.

The people are primarily of African, Madagascan, Indian and Malay heritages. There are some Arabs and a tiny French minority. Islam is the official religion and there is only a small number of Christians. French and Arabic are the official languages, but Comorian is most commonly spoken.

The original inhabitants are believed to have come from Africa. Arabs established sultantates on the islands in the fifteenth century A.D. Various Europeans visited the islands during the next century but they made no claims. France purchased the island of Mayotte in 1841. It declared the other islands a protectorate in 1886. They were a colony administered from Madagascar after 1912. French investors established vanilla and cacao plantations.

Britain occupied Comoros during World War II. In 1958 they became a French Overseas Territory, with partial self-government in 1961. When the other islands voted for independence in 1974, Mayotte remained French. The Comoros Chamber of Deputies declared independence as the Federal Islamic Republic of Comoros on July 6, 1975.

Ahmed Abdallah Abderrahman, the first president, was deposed in a 1976 coup. He staged his own coup two years later and returned to the presidency. He put down a third coup in 1983, but was assassinated in 1989.

Saïd Mohammed Djohar was elected at free elections in 1990 and impeached one year later. With French support Djohar was reinstated. The French put down a coup attempt in 1995.

The islands of Nzwani and Mwali declared independence from the country in 1997. This provoked violence across the country, until an agreement was reached giving the two islands more internal authority. The country's name became the Union of Comoros.

A military coup took place in 1999. Colonel Azali Assoumani took over as president. The following year his forces stopped another coup attempt. Comoros remains one of the poorest countries in the world.

GOVERNMENT
Capital Moroni
Type of government
Transitional government
Independence from France
July 6, 1975
Voting Universal adult suffrage
Head of state President
Head of government Prime Minister
Constitution 1992, 1996, 2001
Legislature
Bicameral Parliament
Federal Assembly (lower house)
Senate (upper house)
Judiciary Supreme Court
Member of IMF, OAU, UN, UNESCO, WHO

LAND AND PEOPLE
Land area 719 sq mi (1862 sq km)
Highest point
Kartala 7,746 ft (2360 m)
Coastline 217 mi (349 km)
Population 614,382
Major cities and populations
Moroni 34,000
Mutsamudu 20,000
Ethnic groups
African, Madagascan, Malay, Indian
Religions Islam 99%,
Christianity 1%
Languages
French, Arabic, Comorian
(all official)

ECONOMIC
Currency Comoros franc
Industry
tourism, perfume distillation
Agriculture
vanilla, cloves, perfume essences, copra, coconuts, bananas, tapioca
Natural resources

Congo

DEMOCRATIC REPUBLIC OF THE CONGO

Formerly Zaire, the Democratic Republic of the Congo is a large country in central Africa. It is dominated by the basin of the Congo River. The northern region is thickly forested and swampy, while most of the south is grassland. The eastern Mitumba Mountain Range rise to more than 16,000 feet (app. 5,000 m). The northern climate is hot and humid all year round. The south's wet and dry seasons are more defined and temperature ranges are greater.

The largest group of people are the Bantu who make up about forty percent of the population. The 200 different ethnic groups include the Azande, Banda, Abarmbo and Pygmy. Large numbers of Hutu refugees fled to the Congo from fighting in Rwanda and Burundi. Half of the population is Christian, while many still practice traditional animist faiths. French is the official language. Kiswahili, Tshiluba, Kikonga and Lingala are also widely spoken.

Pygmies inhabited the region well before the first millennium B.C. Gradually, they were displaced by Bantu peoples from neighboring countries. Bantu began mining copper in the eighth century A.D. They developed a government system and founded the state of Kongo in the fourteenth century.

Portuguese explorer Diogo Cam arrived in 1482. Europeans set up a major slave trading operation, assisted by the local kingdoms. By the seventeenth century, demand for slaves in Brazil had dramatically reduced the population. In the last half of the nineteenth century, much of the eastern region was ruled by Muhammad bin Hamad, an Arab Swahili trader.

King Leopold II of Belgium decided to establish his own colony in the Congo region. He commissioned American explorer Henry Stanley to establish stations along the Congo River and negotiate 'treaties' with local rulers in 1878. Seven years later Leopold established the Congo Free State, a royal colony beyond the control of the Belgian government.

Local natives were forced to work on Leopold's rubber plantations for twenty years. Those who resisted were massacred. The king accumulated a fortune from his Congo holdings. European outrage forced Leopold to hand the colony over to his parliament in 1908. It became a colony known as the Belgian Congo.

Belgium's new control was only slightly less brutal than it had been under the king. Christian missionaries were responsible for most education and social development. Mean-

GOVERNMENT
Capital Kinshasa
Type of government
Transitional military regime
Independence from Belgium
June 30, 1960
Voting
Universal compulsory adult suffrage
Head of state President
Head of government President
Constitution 1967, being redeveloped
Legislature
Transitional Constituent Assembly (appointed by president)
Judiciary Supreme Court
Member of IMF, OAU, UN, UNESCO, UNHCR, WHO, WTO

LAND AND PEOPLE
Land area 905,564 sq mi (2,345,409 sq km)
Highest point Pic Marguerite 16,765 ft (5110 m)
Coastline 21 mi (37 km)
Population 55,225,478
Major cities and populations
Kinshasa 4,600,000
Lubumbashi 851,000
Ethnic groups
Bantu 40%, others 60%
Religions
Christianity 70%, animism 30%
Languages
French (official), indigenous languages

ECONOMIC
Currency Congolese franc
Industry
mining, textiles, footwear, processed foods, beverages, cement
Agriculture
coffee, sugar, palm oil, rubber, tea, quinine, tapioca, bananas, root crops, corn, fruits; timber
Natural resources
cobalt, copper, cadmium, petroleum, diamonds, gold, silver, zinc, manganese, tin, germanium, uranium, bauxite, iron ore, coal, timber

Democratic Republic of the Congo

while, the economy became heavily reliant on gold, copper and diamond mining.

Pro-independence movements were led by Joseph Kasavubu and Patrice Lumumba during the 1950s. Riots broke out in Leopoldville (now Kinshasa) in 1959. The Belgians abandoned the colony on June 30, 1960. Lumumba became premier.

The army mutinied almost immediately. The mineral-rich Katanga province seceded, led by Moïse Tshombe and encouraged by Belgian business interests. The infrastructure collapsed when most Belgian civil servants and administrators departed.

The United Nations sent a peacekeeping force to the Congo in July of 1960. Lumumba asked the Soviet Union for help in reclaiming Katanga. He was deposed by Colonel Joseph-Desire Mobuto under suspicious circumstances. Lumumba was handed over to his Katangan enemies in early 1961 and assassinated.

Turmoil continued. The United States supplied arms to the government forces and white mercenaries were recruited to maintain control. Mobutu dismissed the civilian government and declared himself president in November of 1965.

Mobutu renamed the country Zaïre and began nationalizing key industries after six years in office. European investors were expelled in 1974. Mobutu was unable to lure them back when he realized his mistake. His rule was unshaken by many attempted coups between 1975 and 1978.

Opposition political parties were permitted in 1990. The following year the army rebelled because it had not been paid. Zaïre was slowly collapsing. Rebels took control of the eastern Congo and Kinshasa while Mobutu was hospitalized in Europe. Rebel leader Laurent Kabila renamed the country the Democratic Republic of Congo.

Soldiers in the east rebelled against Kabilla's rule in 1998. Rwanda and Uganda supported the rebels while Zimbabwe, Namibia and Angola assisted Kabila. A cease-fire was negotiated in July 1999. A United Nations peacekeeping force was unable to enter the unstable country. Kabila was assassinated in early 2001 and replaced by his son Major-General Joseph Kabila.

A dusty rural road in the Democratic Republic of the Congo.

Congo

REPUBLIC OF THE CONGO

The Republic of the Congo is located in western Africa. Its two major plateaus run east to west in the center of the country. Most of the landscape is covered with dense tropical rainforest. The climate is equatorial, with little change in high temperatures through the year. The wet season runs from November to April.

Half of the nation's people are Kongo, mostly congregated in the south. People of the north include the Sangha and M'bochi. The population is almost equally split between traditional animist religions and Christianity. French is the official language, but Mono Kutuba and Lingala are widely spoken.

The original Pygmy inhabitants were joined by Bakongo, Sanga and Bateke peoples in the fifteenth century. Portuguese explorer Diogo Cam arrived in 1482 and Europeans quickly established a major slave trading center.

French explorer Pierre Savorgnan de Brazza negotiated treaties with local tribes. The region, known as Middle Congo, was incorporated into French Equatorial Africa in 1883. French companies began rubber and ivory trading.

Growing concern in France over the cruel treatment of laborers prompted more government involvement. The Congo was made a colony in 1910. A bloody uprise staged an uprising in 1928 because abuse of laborers had continued.

Free French forces controlled the Congo during World War II. It was granted internal self-government in 1946. Full autonomy within the French Community came in 1958, followed by independence on August 15, 1960.

Fulbert Youlou, the first president, was forced from office three years later. His replacement, Alphonse Massamba-Débat, tried to restructure the government as a communist state.

Marien Ngouabi became president following a military coup in 1968. He established a one-party state which was more communist than the former government. He changed the country's name to the People's Republic of the Congo. Ngouabi was assassinated in 1977.

President Joachim Yhombi-Opango ruled for two years until Colonel Sassou-Nguesso restored military control. The name of the country was changed back to the Republic of the Congo. Pascal Lissouba won the election in 1992 amid charges of voter fraud.

Civil war erupted in 1997. Forces led by former president Sassou-Nguesso captured the capital, Brazzaville, in October 1997. He established a multi-party cabinet to govern the country.

Cook Islands

The Cook Islands are in the South Pacific Ocean, northeast of New Zealand, between French Polynesia and Fiji. Originally formed by volcanic activity, there are fifteen major islands. They are divided into two distinct groups: the Southern, or Lower, Cook Islands and the Northern Cook Islands. The moderate tropical climate is often affected by cyclones between November and March.

Most Cook Islanders are of Polynesian descent. Christianity is the religion of the majority. The official language is English, but many people speak Cook Island Maori.

The people of the Cook Islands rely upon income from tourism. Earnings from the export of fruits, fish and black pearls is also significant.

The islands were first settled in the sixth century A.D. The Polynesian peoples migrated by boat from other Pacific island groups. They lived an idyllic life, interrupted by occasional internal disputes.

It is believed that Spanish ships visited the islands in the late sixteenth century. British navigator Captain James Cook arrived in 1773. This was the last anyone saw of Europeans until missionaries from London arrived in 1821. Christianity quickly took hold of the culture, a grip it retains today.

Britain declared the islands a protectorate in 1888, largely to thwart French expansionism. The British Colonial Office transferred administration to its New Zealand colony in 1901. Independence came in August of 1965.

The Cook Islands opted to become self-governing in free association with New Zealand. All defense and foreign relations matters are handled by New Zealand. Prime Minister Sir Albert Henry led the country until 1978 when he was accused of fraud. Two subsequent leaders have also been removed from office. Dr. Robert Wooten was appointed Prime Minister in 2002.

Aitutaki Lagoon

LONELY PLANET IMAGES – PETER HENDRIE

Costa Rica

REPUBLIC OF COSTA RICA

GOVERNMENT
Website www.casapres.go.cr
Capital San José
Type of government Republic
Independence from Spain 1823
Voting
Universal adult suffrage, compulsory
Head of state President
Head of government President
Constitution 1949
Legislature
Unicameral Legislative Assembly
Judiciary Supreme Court
Member of
IMF, OAS, UN, UNESCO, WHO, WTO

LAND AND PEOPLE
Land area 19,730 sq mi (51,100 sq km)
Highest point Cerro Chirripo 12,530 ft (3,819 m)
Coastline 804 mi (1290 km)
Population 3,834,935
Major cities and populations
San José 975,000
Ethnic groups
European 80%, African 2%, indigenous 1%, others 17%
Religions Christianity
Languages
Spanish (official)

ECONOMIC
Currency Costa Rican colon
Industry
coffee, pineapples, bananas, sugar, corn, rice, beans, potatoes, beef, timber
Agriculture
wheat, barley, sugar cane, fruits, beef cattle, sheep, wool, poultry, dairy
Natural resources timber

Tiny Costa Rica covers only 19,730 square miles (51,100 sq km) in Central America. The Caribbean Sea is on the east coast and the Pacific Ocean borders the west. Much of the landscape is rugged volcanic ranges running north and south. The Caribbean coastline is heavily forested. The coastal climate is tropical with regular rainfall. In the interior, conditions are more temperate.

Eighty percent of the population has Spanish heritage. Some indigenous peoples live in the far south. Almost everyone is Roman Catholic. Spanish is the official language.

Costa Rican civilization stretches back 10,000 years. Incan and Mayan cultures were major influences. The first European visitor was Christopher Columbus in 1502, who named the area Costa Rica, or Rich Coast.

Indigenous resistance prevented permanent Spanish settlement before 1563. Diseases brought from Europe eventually reduced the population, destroying opposition and limiting opportunities for an agricultural system dependent upon ingenous people for slave labor.

Costa Rica was part of Spain's Guatemala captaincy-general. Spanish rule over the area ended in 1823. Costa Rica became part of Mexico briefly, then it was one of the United Provinces of Central America. It gained independence in 1838.

Coffee growing became the mainstay of the economy. The United Fruit Company introduced banana cultivation in Limón province using imported West Indian laborers in 1874. Railroad and communication systems were constructed.

President Alfredo Gonzáles was deposed by Federico Tinoco in 1917. With United States backing, the people overthrew Tinoco two years later. Disputes over presidential election results provoked a six-week-long civil war in 1948. The subsequent junta, led by José Figueres Ferrer, disbanded the military. This has ensured a relatively stable democratic government.

A new constitution was proclaimed in 1949, with Otilio Ulate as president. A number of moderate governments that followed helped to make Costa Rica the most democratic country in Central America.

Economic recessions and disastrous volcanic eruptions in 1963 and 1968 caused serious problems for Costa Ricans. A number of drug-related kidnappings stirred controversy in the mid-1990s. Nonetheless, its stable democracy has made Costa Rica a favorite holiday destination, particularly for North Americans.

Côte d'Ivoire

REPUBLIC OF CÔTE d'IVOIRE

Côte d'Ivoire is a small country in western Africa. The narrow, sandy coastal strip in the south gives way to tropical forests inland. Much of the forest has been cleared for farmland. The northern part of the country is a plateau covered with some glassland. The climate varies from the high rainfall of the tropical coast to the drier, more temperate north.

Of the more than sixty ethnic groups, the largest are the Baule, Anyi, Bete and Kru in the south and the Senufo, Malinke and Mande in the north. More than half the population follows traditional animist religions. A quarter are Muslims and the rest are Christians. French is the official language. A wide variety of African dialects are also in use.

Many distinct kingdoms were established in the Côte d'Ivoire region between the sixteenth and nineteenth centuries. The Kru came from Liberia, the Mande from Guinea and the Baule from Ghana.

French missionaries were the first Europeans to arrive in the 1600s. In later years Spanish, British, French and Portuguese slave and ivory traders built settlements on the coast.

France became the dominant power after 1840. It established Côte d'Ivoire as a colony in 1893 made it a part of

French West Africa in 1904. Resistance from the Malinke and Baule was finally subdued in 1908.

The region became a major producer of cacao and coffee, using forced labor, after World War I. Côte d'Ivoire chose autonomy within the French Community in 1958. It declared itself independent two years later.

President Félix Houphouët-Boigny maintained a dialogue with apartheid South Africa. This made Côte d'Ivoire unpopular with other African nations. The nation was a one-party state until 1990 when Houphouët-Boigny won a seventh term.

His successor, Henri Konan Bédié, followed a policy of privatization and economic reform. When unpaid soldiers rioted in Abidjan in 1999, General Robert Gueï assumed power after a coup d'état.

Laurent Gbagbo was elected in 2000 but Gueï prevented him from taking office. Gueï backed down following protests by police and military. Battles erupted between southern Christians and northern Muslims at the same time.

Gbagbo's unpopular presidency led to a military coup in September of 2002. Although initially unsuccessful, the various factions continue to fight for control of the nation.

GOVERNMENT
Capital Yamoussoukro
Type of government Republic
Independence from France
August 7, 1960
Voting Universal adult suffrage
Head of state President
Head of government Prime Minister
Constitution 1960
Legislature
Unicameral National Assembly
Judiciary Supreme Court
Member of IMF, OAU, UN, UNESCO, UNHCR, WHO, WTO

LAND AND PEOPLE
Land area 124,504 sq mi
(322,463 sq km)
Highest point Mont Nimba
5,676 ft (1,752 m)
Coastline 321 mi (515 km)
Population 16,804,784
Major cities and populations
Abidjan 2,500,000
Bouaké 320,000
Yamoussoukro 110,000
Ethnic groups
Baule 25%, Bete 20%, Senufo 15%,
Malinke 12%, others 28%
Religions Traditional animism
60%, Islam 25%, Christianity 12%,
Languages
French (official), indigenous languages

ECONOMIC
Currency CFA franc
Industry
foodstuffs, beverages, wood products, oil refining, motor vehicles, textiles, fertilizer, chemicals, mining
Agriculture
coffee, cacao beans, bananas, palm kernels, corn, rice, tapioca, sweet potatoes, sugar, cotton, rubber, timber
Natural resources
petroleum, natural gas, diamonds, manganese, iron ore, cobalt, bauxite, copper

Croatia

REPUBLIC OF CROATIA

GOVERNMENT
Website www.vlada.hr
Capital Zagreb
Type of government Republic
Separation from Yugoslavia
June 22, 1991
Voting Universal adult suffrage
Head of state President
Head of government Prime
Minister
Constitution 1990
Legislature
Unicameral Assembly (Sabor)
Judiciary Supreme Court
Member of
CE, IMF, UN, UNESCO, WHO, WTO

LAND AND PEOPLE
Land area 21,800 sq mi
(56,461 sq km)
Highest point Dinara 6,003 ft
(1830 m)
Coastline 3,626 mi (5,835 km)
Population 4,390,751
Major cities and populations
Zagreb 950,000
Split 215,000
Rijeka 210,000
Ethnic groups
Croat 90%, Serbian 10%
Religions Christianty 90%,
Islam 3%
Languages Croatian (official)

ECONOMIC
Currency Kuna
Industry
mining, chemicals, plastics,
machine tools, electronics, pig iron,
rolled steel, aluminum, paper, wood
products, textiles, shipbuilding,
petroleum refining, food, beverages,
tourism
Agriculture
wheat, corn, beet sugar, sunflower
seed, barley, alfalfa, olives, citrus,
grapes, soybeans, potatoes, dairy
Natural resources
oil, coal, bauxite, iron ore, calcium,
natural asphalt, silica, mica, clays,
salt

Previously part of Yugoslavia, Croatia is located in eastern Europe. The west country, also known as Dalmatia, is barren and rocky, dominated by the Dinaric Alps. The eastern inland is lower-lying agricultural land drained by the Drava and Sava rivers. One-third of the landscape is heavily forested. The coastal climate is Mediterranean. Inland, it tends to be cooler with freezing temperatures in winter.

The people are predominantly ethnic Croats. There is a Serbian minority of just over ten percent. Their numbers dropped dramatically during the forced evictions of the 1990s. All but ten percent of the population is Christian. Three quarters of these are Catholic, the rest are Eastern Orthodox. There is a tiny Muslim minority. Croatian is the language most commonly used.

Croatia was originally a part of the Roman Empire, within the province of Pannonia. The Croat peoples arrived in the seventh century A.D. Within two centuries they had converted to Christianity. In the tenth century the coastal lands of Dalmatia were incorporated into the kingdom, despite opposition from Venice.

Hungary gained control of Croatia in the late eleventh century. King Ladislaus I of Hungary deposed the Croatian monarchy and established links with the various tribal groups. Croatia was permitted a monarch who was subservient to Hungary's king.

Hungary was replaced by the Turkish Ottoman Empire in 1526. The Hungarians were

A man returns to his home after it was destroyed in the worst of the fighting in the mid-1990s.

Croatia

driven out in the seventeenth century by the Austrian Habsburg Empire. This was formalized under the Treaty of Carlowitz in 1699. Croatia came under French control for a time, during the Napoleonic Wars.

When Habsburg control was reasserted, Croatia declared itself independent in 1848. This did not last. Soon Croatia was assigned to Hungarian control by the Habsburgs. The people of Croatia were feeling relatively self-sufficient by the 1870s, but they still felt a good deal of influence from Hungary.

The Habsburg territories of Serbia, Montenegro and Slovenia joined Croatia as a single country after World War I. The new nation was called Yugoslavia, beginning in 1929.

Croatia was unhappy with the centralized structure that subsequently developed. Vladimir Maek approached Mussolini in 1939 seeking Italian assistance in gaining Croatia's independence. It did not happen, but the country did gain a stronger identity within Yugoslavia.

When Germany invaded Yugoslavia in 1941, the fascist Ustachi movement seized power. Two hundred thousand-

Serbs, Jews and Gypsies, as well as Croatian opponents, were exterminated under its brutal rule. Many more were sent to concentration camps. The oppressed population sided with anti-fascist partisans led by Marshal Josip Broz Tito. He formed a communist government for Yugoslavia, with Croatia as a member in 1945.

The Yugoslav government responded to flourishing Croatian nationalism by granting it a degree of autonomy in the 1970s. A non-communist provincial government was elected in 1990. The following year Croatia declared itself independent of Yugoslavia. Franjo Tudjman became the new president.

Yugoslav troops, mostly of Serbian ethnic background, attempted to regain control of Croatia. At least 6,000 people were killed and 23,000 wounded in the battles that followed. The United Nations arranged a truce in early 1992 and sent in a peacekeeping force.

Croatian forces recaptured most Serb-held territory in 1995. The last region, Slavonia, was returned to Croatia in 1998, ending the civil war that had continued on a smaller scale.

Following Tudjman's death, Vlatko Pavletic was named acting president. Stipe Mesi was elected national leader in 2002. The new administration marked a change to a more moderate system. Croatia continues to rebuild. It is one of the more economically successful countries which emerged from the former Yugoslavia.

A United Nations peacekeeping force helicopter crew surveys a damaged factory in 1996.

Cuba

REPUBLIC OF CUBA

Cuba is located in the Caribbean Sea, just south of Florida. Three sets of mountains on the main island run east to west. The southern and western coastlines are dotted with marshes. The rest of the landscape is mainly lowlands and about thirty percent is forested. The subtropical climate is warm and humid year round. The rainy season usually occurs from May to October.

Most Cubans are descended from either Spanish or African ancestors. Many are a combination of both. Christianity is tolerated by the communist government. Spanish, the official language, is most commonly used.

The original Ciboney peoples were displaced by Arawak immigrants from Haiti. Christopher Columbus landed on Cuba in 1492. No colonial activity occurred until 1511, when a permanent settlement was established at Baracoa. The small indigenous population was quickly wiped out.

Cuba became a staging post for treasure fleets sailing to Spain. Sugar plantations were established using slave labor from Africa. Cuban ports were under almost constant attack by French and British pirates.

Briefly under British control in 1762, Cuba reverted to Spain under the Treaty of Paris the following year. Harsh Spanish rulers worked to develop both commerce and agriculture. The slave trade flourished in the first half of the nineteenth century.

Various rebellions culminated in 1868 when plantation owner Carlos de Céspedes declared Cuba independent. The guerrilla war against Spain was known as the Ten Years' War. It ended in an 1878 peace treaty which promised reform and self-government, but neither ever took place.

Writer José Martí began a war of independence in 1895. Spain responded brutally. When the American navy ship USS Maine was blown up in Havana harbor in 1898, the United States blamed Spain. U.S. forces landed quickly. Spain surrendered control. The American military ruled the island until 1902 when the republic formally began.

Estrada Palma became the first president, but the United States retained the right to intervene in Cuban affairs. American economic dominance provoked a revolution in 1906. It was suppressed by United States forces, who remained for three years. Cuba entered World War I in 1917 on the side of the Allies.

Gerardo Machado became president in 1924. He promoted industrial and agricultural development and public works. He soon became obsessed with elim-

Cuba

Transport, Havana style — a bictaxi and one of the thousands of well-preserved 1950s American cars, in this case a Chrysler.

inating opponents and was overthrown by the military in 1933.

Coup leader Fulgencio Batista installed a puppet president controlled by the military. Between 1940 and 1944 he assumed the presidency.

Cuba entered World War II in 1941. It became a charter member of the United Nations. After the war, Cuba also joined the Organization of American States (OAS)

A string of corrupt leaders gave the army consistent reason to become involved in the government. Batista was brought back to power after a March 1952 coup. His links with American organized crime grew rapidly.

Batista's savage crushing of any opposition greatly

increased the popularity of rebel leader Fidel Castro. Batista fled the country and victorious rebel forces marched into Havana on January 1, 1959. Castro took power one month later, trying and executing over 500 Batista supporters.

Foreign-owned businesses were nationalized and opponents of the new government eliminated. Medical care and education for all the population were quickly introduced. Although it severed diplomatic relations in 1961, the United States retained its Guantanamo naval base on Cuban soil.

Alliances with the Soviet Union and other eastern European communist countries were established. The United States responded with a trade

embargo. A direct military intervention, the Bay of Pigs invasion, was a disaster.

The Soviet Union began building missile bases in Cuba in October, 1962. The U.S. Navy blockaded Cuban ports, provoking a confrontation between U.S. President Kennedy and Soviet Premier Khrushchev. After a period of great tension, the Soviet Union withdrew its missiles.

Cuba was often accused to trying to stimulate revolutionary wars in South American countries during the 1960s. The country was subsequently expelled from the OAS. Cuba became involved in aiding African and Middle Eastern rebel groups in the 1970s.

With the collapse of the Soviet Union, its aid to Cuba ended. Many countries have resumed diplomatic relations with Cuba, despite U. S. objections. Tourism, especially from Europe, rose dramatically in the 1990s. The United States' embargo remains in place.

Cyprus

REPUBLIC OF CYPRUS

GOVERNMENT
Website www.pio.gov.cy
Capital Nicosia
Type of government Republic
Independence from Britain
August 16, 1960
Voting Universal adult suffrage
Head of state President
Head of government President
Constitution 1960
Legislature
Unicameral House
of Representatives
Judiciary Supreme Court
Member of
CN, IMF, UN, UNESCO, WHO, WTO

LAND AND PEOPLE
Land area 3,572 sq mi
(9,251 sq km)
Highest point
Olympus 6,321 ft (1951 m)
Coastline 404 mi (648 km)
Population 767,314
Major cities and populations
Nicosia 155,000
Limassol 115,000
Larnaca 51,000
Ethnic groups Greek Cypriot 75%,
Turkish Cypriot 20%, others 5%
Religions Christianity 80%, Islam
20%
Languages
Greek, Turkish (both official)

ECONOMIC
Currency Cypriot pound
Industry
food, beverages, textiles, chemicals,
metal products, tourism, wood
products
Agriculture
potatoes, citrus, vegetables, barley,
grapes, olives, vegetables
Natural resources
copper, pyrites, asbestos, gypsum,
timber, salt, marble, clay

Cyprus is an island just south of Turkey in the eastern Mediterranean Sea. The Kyrenian Mountains run along the northern coast. These give way to the Mesaoria Plain and the Troodos Mountains farther south. Just under twenty percent of Cyprus is forested. The climate is Mediterranean with hot summers and mild winters.

Around seventy-five percent of Cypriots have Greek background, while twenty percent are Turkish. They practice either the Greek Orthodox or the Sunni Muslim faith. Greek and Turkish are the official languages.

An early civilization existed from 6000 to 3000 B.C. Greeks migrated there around 1500 B.C., followed by Phoenicians in 800 B.C. It fell to Alexander the Great's invasion in 333 B.C..

The island was part of the Roman Empire from 58 B.C. to A.D. 395. A long period of control by the Byzantine Empire ended with the 1191 invasion by Christian crusaders. Venice took control in 1489, replaced in 1571 by the Turkish Ottoman Empire.

Having controlled Cyprus since 1878, Britain formally annexed it during World War I. It became a crown colony in 1925. The majority Greek Cypriot population wanted union with Greece. Turkish Cypriots demanded the island be partitioned along ethnic lines.

Terrorist actions erupted in 1955, spearheaded by Colonel George Grivas' EOKA organization. Britain deported Archbishop Makarios III, spiritual leader of the Greek Cypriots, in 1956. Cyprus became independent in August of 1960. It was not united with Greece nor was it partitioned. Makarios became president.

A United Nations peacekeeping force arrived in 1965, in response to Greek-Turkish friction. It remains in place today.

Police launched an attack on the EOKA movement on July 15, 1974. The national guard overthrew Makarios, who fled the country. Nikos Sampson became president. On July 20, Turkish troops occupied one-third of the island, expelling Greek Cypriots from this enclave. Sampson's regime collapsed and a United Nations cease-fire took effect on July 22. Makarios returned as president in 1975, dying in office two years later.

Turkish Cypriots declared their section of the island the Turkish Republic of Northern Cyprus in 1983. Turkey has boosted the Turkish Cypriot population by sending immigrants to the island. In early 2003, there was growing agitation on both sides to end the partition of the island.

Czech Republic

The Czech Republic is the western portion of the area that was previously Czechoslovakia. It is a land-locked country in central Europe.

The landscape in the west is marked by the Bohemian Plateau, which runs from the Sudeten Mountains in the north to the Moravian lowlands in the south. The lower-lying Bohemian Basin, through which the Elbe-Moldau river system flows, is found in the east.

The climate is continental. Winters can be cold, with the average January temperature of 30° F. ª(-1° C.). Summers are much warmer, with a July average of 67° F (19.4° C.). In the more mountainous regions averages drop significantly. Much of the annual rainfall occurs in summer.

Close to ninety-five percent of the people are ethnic Czechs. There are minorities of Slovaks, Poles, Germans and Hungarians and a small community of Gypsies. Although there is no official religion, the Czech Republic is regarded as Christian. Czech, written with the Roman alphabet, it the official language. Slovak is also spoken by a large number of the people.

The Czech economy was under firm state control until the end of the 1980s. When the communist government collapsed, the nation converted rapidly and painlessly to a market economy. Prosperity in the early 1990s gave way to economic slowdown later on.

Agricultural products include wheat, barley, rye, beet sugar, corn and potatoes. The country is heavily industrialized. Iron and steel are produced in the Moravia region. Other major manufacturing includes motor vehicles, machinery, chemicals, glass and electronics. There are very few significant mineral resources.

The president is elected by the parliament for a five-year term. He appoints the prime minister and cabinet. The bicameral legislature consists of the Senate and the Chamber of Deputies. Senators are elected for two-, four- or six-year terms. Deputies are elected for four-year terms. Both houses are chosen in a popular vote by the Czech people.

There is evidence that people lived in the Czech Republic in 4000 B.C. It is known that Celtic tribes inhabited the region around 400 B.C. They were displaced by the Marcomanni, a Germanic tribe. By the seventh century A.D., the region was populated by people of Slav origin, the ancestors of today's Czechs. They converted to Christianity 200 years later.

The regions of Moravia and Bohemia were well established by the eleventh century A.D. Immigrants flowed in from German areas. The Czech King Charles IV was crowned Holy Roman Emperor in 1346.

As in many other parts of Europe, there was a popular

FLAT EARTH PICTURE GALLERY

Prague's Wenceslas Square

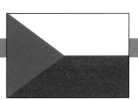

movement toward religious reform in the fifteenth century, led by Jan Hus. It soon encompassed nationalism as well as religion. Hus' execution provoked decades of civil war. The Austrian Habsburg dynasty took control in the early 1500s. A revolt against the Habsburgs was defeated in the Battle of White Mountain in 1620. People were forced to adopt Catholicism and German culture.

Freedom from Habsburg domination came in 1918 with the collapse of the Austro-Hungarian Empire. The Czech region was united with Slovakia on November 14, 1918, under the Treaty of St. Germain. It was an unusual union, given the very different backgrounds of the Czech and Slovak peoples. Much of the industrial strength of the Austro-Hungarian Empire was inherited.

Problems of unity were, to some extent, overcome by the quality of Czechoslovakia's leadership. The first president was Thomas Masaryk. Governments in the 1920s and 1930s were coalitions. They embraced all political parties except the communists.

The highly centralized nature of the government led to resentment in many regions. This ill-feeling increased during the Depression of the 1930s when the ethnically German Sudetenland industrial areas were badly affected. A separatist movement, led by Konrad Henlein, emerged. It was encouraged by Nazi Germany after 1933. The failure of the Czech central government to grant self-government to provinces did not help matters.

Henlein demanded the ethnically German regions of Czechoslovakia be allowed to unite with Germany. German Chancellor Adolf Hitler exploited this. He threatened war if Henlein's demands were not met. The Allies, particularly Britain and France, caved in and abandoned Czechoslovakia in late 1938. Germany occupied the Sudetenland.

Czech President Eduard Benes resigned, to be replaced by a fervently pro-German leadership. The entire country was surrendered to German control in March of 1939, although Slovakia was more or less independent. The province of Ruthenia was handed over to Hungary.

Benes set up a government-in-exile in London when World War II broke out. It was recognized by the Allies as the official government of Czechoslovakia in 1941. Forces from the Soviet Union and the United States engaged the German military in Czechoslovakia in April 1944. They entered

Czech Republic

Prague on May 12, 1945, the end of the war in Europe.

The liberators were supported by an uprising of Czech people. Benes reached an agreement with the Czech communists to form a government. Allied occupation forces were withdrawn at the end of 1945. The Allies' Potsdam Conference agreed to the expulsion of three-million Germans from Czechoslovakia. All pre-war territory, except Ruthenia, was restored.

Communists gained the largest number of votes at the May 1946 general election. They became the dominant force in the governing National Front coalition. Benes was

elected president. When the communists brought forward a new constitution in 1948, Benes chose to resign rather than agree to it. He was followed by other non-communist ministers.

Czechoslovakia moved rapidly toward becoming a communist state. Industry was nationalized and various freedoms curtailed. Riots over the weakening economy in 1953 sparked a modest program of reforms. Most were reversed four years later.

A constitution based on Soviet ideas came into effect in 1960. Another reform movement was gathering support within four years. Media controls were eased and cultural activities liberalized.

President Antonin Novotný was constantly criticized for ignoring the Slovak minority. He was replaced in four years by Alexander Dubcek, a Slovak, as leader of the communist party. Ludvik Svoboda became president, setting the stage for what would be called the Prague Spring.

Widespread liberalizations included the abolition of censorship, self-government for Slovakia and guarantees of human rights. This greatly alarmed the Soviet Union. On August 20, Soviet tanks and infantry

The Charles Bridge in Prague, the capital of the Czech Republic.

invaded Czechoslovakia. Dubcek was arrested and sent to Moscow.

Reforms were severely curtailed. Dubcek's leadership lasted only until April 1969. After he was deposed, the harsh and repressive ways of the communist state returned. All dissent was ruthlessly crushed.

Demand for reform grew throughout the 1980s. Anti-government demonstrations became common, particularly in Prague. The protests continued, leading to the government's collapse in November.

The new non-communist leader was former dissident Václav Havel. The following year his administration began privatizing state-controlled industries. Economic systems were freed up and foreign investment encouraged. Called the Velvet Revolution, the change was profound at all levels of society.

The Slovakian secession movement achieved its aim on August 26, 1992. The Czech Republic and Slovakia became separate nations on January 1, 1993. The Czech Republic, despite continuing economic problems, continues its rapid emergence from the communist years. It joined the North Atlantic Treaty Organization (NATO) in 1999. The Social Democratic Party won the elections of 2002.

Denmark

KINGDOM OF DENMARK

GOVERNMENT
Website www.folketinget.dk
Capital Copenhagen
Type of government
Constitutional monarchy
Voting Universal adult suffrage
Head of state Monarch
Head of government Prime
Minister
Constitution 1849, revised 1953
Legislature
Unicameral Parliament (Folketing)
Judiciary Supreme Court
Member of EU, IMF, NATO, OECD,
UN, UNESCO, UNHCR, WHO, WTO

LAND AND PEOPLE
Land area 16,639 sq mi
(43,094 sq km)
Highest point Yding Skovhoej
561 ft (173 m)
Coastline 4,557 mi (7,314 km)
Population 5,368,854
Major cities and populations
Copenhagen 1,375,000
Aarhus 280,000
Odense 190,000
Ethnic groups
Danish 92%, German 2%, others 6%
Religion Christianity 94%,
Islam 2%, Judaism 1%
Languages
Danish (official), indigenous
languages

ECONOMIC
Currency Krone
Industry
tourism, food processing,
machinery, textiles, clothing,
chemicals, electronics, wood
products, shipbuilding
Agriculture
barley, wheat, potatoes, beet sugar,
pork, dairy, seafood
Natural resources
petroleum, natural gas,
seafood, salt, limestone

Southernmost of the Scandinavian countries, Denmark occupies the Jutland Peninsula in northern Europe. It also includes almost 500 islands, the largest being Sjælland, Lolland, Falster and Funen. The self-governing dependencies of Faeroe Islands and Greenland are also part of Denmark.

In the west, most of the country is low-lying with sandy soil. More than sixty percent of the fertile eastern plains are cultivated. Denmark has a temperate climate affected by the Gulf Stream. Winters are cold, summers are mild to warm. When the Baltic Sea is heavily iced, winters can become extremely cold. The heaviest rains fall is in the western part of the country.

Over ninety percent of the population is of Danish descent. There is also a small German minority. Indigenous peoples live on the Faroe Islands and in Greenland. Christianity is the majority religion, with most people being followers of the National Church, the Lutheran Evangelical denomination. There are tiny Muslim and Jewish minorities.

Most Danes speak Danish. There are several dialects which derive from Old Scandinavian. Danish is closely related to Norwegian and Swedish. A German-speaking minority lives in the south. Peoples of the Faroe Islands speak Faeroese, while those of Greenland speak Greenlandic.

Denmark began a determined shift away from agriculture into more manufacturing after World War II. Much of the land is still used for agriculture. Key crops are beet sugar, potatoes, wheat, oats and barley. Pigs, poultry and cattle-raising play a large part in the agricultural sector as well. Denmark has always been a fishing nation, but that industry is presently in decline.

Danish manufacturers produces a large variety of foods, notably dairy products. It is also a leading manufacturer of electronic equipment and components, chemicals, transport equipment, paper, timber goods, machinery and metal goods.

Denmark is a constitutional monarchy, with its most recent constitution adopted in 1953. The hereditary monarch is head of state. As head of government, the prime minister holds office with the support of the parliament, called the Folketing. It is a unicameral body with members elected for a four-year term.

It is believed the Jutland region was settled around 10,000 B.C. It was not until the fifth century B.C. that the inhabitants made an impact on the larger world as Vikings.

Denmark

During the following centuries, Viking warriors invaded many parts of Europe, gaining a reputation for maritime ability and ferocity in battle.

The Viking invasion of Britain in the ninth century A.D. had a profound effect on that island's culture. Christianity was introduced about the same time. For a brief time in the eleventh century, Norway and England were united with Denmark.

Parts of southern Sweden were incorporated into Denmark until the seventeenth century. From 1157 to 1241 Denmark controlled much of northern Europe. It went through its own Lutheran Reformation in the mid-1500s.

The present Danish royal house of Oldenburg was established in 1448 when Christian I ascended the throne. Danish supremacy ended at the hands of Sweden, when it was humiliated in the Thirty Years War (1618-48), which was fought over religious differences.

The sixteenth century marked the beginning of a period of considerable intellectual and artistic development. It was also a time when the country remained separate from conflicts in other parts of Europe. Moves were made to emancipate the peasants who worked the land.

Denmark sided with France during the Napoleonic Wars. As a result, the British navy destroyed much of the Danish fleet. At the end of the wars, the 1814 Treaty of Kiel removed Norway from Denmark's control and gave it to Sweden.

Denmark led the way in developing public education and encouraging the arts in the nineteenth century. At the same time, serfs were emancipated and encouraged to take up their own lands to expand the agricultural industry. These developments culminated in the creation of the democratic constitution of 1849.

The Germanic people of Denmark's Schleswig and Holstein regions rejected the new arrangements and began a campaign to break away. This resulted in a war with Prussia, which Denmark lost in 1864. Both provinces then became part of Germany. Schleswig voted in 1920 to return to Denmark.

Between the two world wars, further changes took place. All adults were granted the right to vote. These advancements accelerated in 1929, following the victory of the Social Democrats led by Prime Minister Thorvald Stauning. Denmark soon developed the sort of welfare state that most European nations did not attempt until after World War II. A new system of progressive taxation was introduced.

Denmark signed a ten-year non-aggression pact with Germany to reaffirm its status as a neutral country during World War II. This failed to protect Denmark from a German inva-

The colorful architecture of Copenhagen's waterfront.

sion in April of 1943. King Christian X remained head of state until August when actions by Danish resistance fighters reached a peak. Martial law was proclaimed and the king was arrested.

In a major humanitarian effort, most of the country's Jewish population was taken to neutral Sweden. This prevented their likely shipment to German extermination camps. British troops liberated the country in May of 1945. The government was resurrected and the Social Democrats took power. Denmark's neutral stance was abandoned when the country joined the North Atlantic Treaty Organization (NATO) in 1949.

The constitution was revamped in 1953 to create a single house of parliament. The royal line of succession was changed to enable women as well as men to become monarch. The social welfare system was improved and refined during the 1950s. When, Danes voted to join the European Economic Community (EEC) in 1972, the issue was hotly debated.

The political system became less stable as more and more independent politicians were elected. A coalition government was formed under the leadership of Poul Schlütter in 1982. It was the first conservative government since 1901.

Denmark experienced economic problems during the 1980s and '90s. Unemployment escalated as did the cost of its social security program. Its foreign debt had grown. Wide-ranging labor market reforms were instituted along with a program to reduce taxation. Despite these problems, years of economic stability have given Danes one of the highest standards of living in the world.

Proposals for further integration with the European community caused serious disagreements during the 1990s. Initially, voters rejected the Maastricht Treaty on European unity in 1992. It was passed once clauses for easy resignation were added. A referendum in September of 2000 resulted in a narrow rejection of the single European currency.

Djibouti

REPUBLIC OF DJIBOUTI

A tiny country of less than 9,000 square miles (app. 23,00 000 sq km), Djibouti is in northeast Africa. It is located on the Strait of Bab al-Mandeb, where the Gulf of Aden meets the Red Sea. The landscape is mostly desert, with the occasional volcanic peaks and a narrow, fertile coastal strip. The climate is consistently hot. The average temperature is 86° F (30°C). Rain, when it does fall, is sparse.

Sixty percent of the population is Somali and thirty-five percent is Afar. There are small groups of Arabs, Ethiopians, Italians and French. Large numbers of Ethiopians fleeing war in their country settled in Djibouti after 1975. The majority of the population is Sunni Muslim, while a small percentage is Christian. The official language is Arabic. French, Somali and Afar are spoken as well.

The region of Djibouti has been inhabited since Paleolithic times. Arab ancestors of the Afar people made it their home in the 200s B. C. They were followed years later by the Somalis. France took possession of the Obock region with the agreement of the local sultan in 1861. It intended to begin commercial competition with Britain's port at Aden.

Djibouti became a colony of French Somaliland in 1888. It was an important fueling and supply center for ships passing through the Suez Canal. A railway was built to Addis Ababa, Ethiopia in 1917. Djibouti became a territory of the French Union in 1946. Membership in the French Community came twelve years later.

The dominant Somali community wanted independence, which France opposed. A deal with the minority Afar for a public decision resulted in a 1967 vote to continue union with France.

Independence finally came ten years later. Hassan Gouled was the first president. Djibouti became a one-party state in 1981. Ethnic friction continued and tensions flared into violence in 1989. An Afar rebellion against the Somali-dominated government raged from 1991 to 1994.

The unemployment rate had climbed to nearly 50 percent by the mid-1990s. The United Nations has estimated that more than ten percent of the population has Acquired Immune Deficiency Syndrome (AIDS) or the virus that causes it.

President Gouled chose not to run for reelection in 1999. His chosen successor, Ismail Guelleh, won a 74 percent majority of the popular vote.

France continues to maintain a strong military presence in the country. Djibouti is an vital shipping port on the route through the Suez Canal.

GOVERNMENT
Capital Djibouti
Type of government Republic
Independence from France
June 27, 1977
Voting Universal adult suffrage
Head of state President
Head of government Prime Minister
Constitution 1992
Legislature
Unicameral Chamber of Deputies
Judiciary Supreme Court
Member of IMF, OAU, UN, UNESCO, WHO, WTO

LAND AND PEOPLE
Land area 8,950 sq mi
(23,200 sq km)
Highest point Moussa Ali
6,570 ft (2,028 m)
Coastline 196 mi (314 km)
Population 472,810
Major cities and populations
Djibouti 390,000
Ethnic groups
Somali 60%, Afar 35%, others 5%
Religions Islam 95%,
Christianity 5%
Languages Arabic (official)

ECONOMIC
Currency Djibouti franc
Industry
agricultural processing
Agriculture
fruits, vegetables, goats, sheep, camels
Natural resources minimal

Dominica

COMMONWEALTH OF DOMINICA

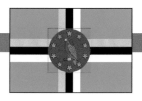

Between the islands of Guadaloupe and Martinique in the Caribbean Sea, Dominica is an island formed by an ancient volcano. It has several mountain peaks rising to more than 4,000 feet (1447 m) above sea level. Dense forest covers almost half of the island. It has a tropical climate with warm to high temperatures and high humidity.

Most of the people are descended from slaves brought from Africa. A small number have indigenous ancestors. The people are predominantly Christians who speak English.

Dominica was first inhabited by Arawak peoples. They were pushed out by Caribs from South America. The island was sighted by Christopher Columbus in 1493. Initial European attempts to establish a settlement failed, due to the resistance of the Caribs.

France established the first settlement on the island in the mid-1700s. The British took possession in 1798. Dominica later became part of the Leeward Islands dependency. The Caribs were all but wiped out during this time. Slaves were brought from Africa to work the British plantations until slavery was abolished in 1833.

The people of Dominica were given voting rights in 1951. The island became self-governing in 1967. Independence from Britain came on November 3, 1978. Patrick John was the first prime minister. The following year Dominica was struck by a major hurricane which killed 50 people and did considerable damage.

The Dominican government gained international notoriety in the late 1990s. Leaders were charged with granting passports to people who invest in the country. This practice resulted in the resignation of the prime minister in 2000 due to popular concerns about the country's image. Dominica remains one of the poorest of the Caribbean islands.

LONELY PLANET IMAGES – NED FRIARY

A typical house in Roseau.

GOVERNMENT
Website www.government.dm
Capital Roseau
Type of government Republic
Independence from Britain
November 3, 1978
Voting Universal adult suffrage
Head of state President
Head of government Prime Minister
Constitution 1978
Legislature
Unicameral House of Assembly
Judiciary
Eastern Caribbean Supreme Court
Member of Caricom, CN, IMF, OAS, UN, UNESCO, WHO, WTO

LAND AND PEOPLE
Land area 290 sq mi (751 sq km)
Highest point Morne Diablatins
4,688 ft (1,447 m)
Coastline 92 mi (148 km)
Population 70,158
Major cities and populations
Roseau 16,000
Ethnic groups African 91%, European-African 6%, indigenous 2%
Religion Christianity
Languages
English (official)

ECONOMIC
Currency East Caribbean dollar
Industry
soap, coconut oil, tourism, copra, furniture, footwear
Agriculture
bananas, citrus, mangoes, root crops, coconuts, cacao
Natural resources
timber, seafood

Dominican Republic

The Dominican Republic occupies the eastern two-thirds of the island of Hispaniola in the Caribbean Sea. Dominating the landscape are the Cordillera Mountains. Between parallel mountain ranges lies the fertile Cibao Valley. The eastern coast is also fertile, well-watered land, but the western areas are generally quite arid. The wet season runs from May to November. The island lies within the region's hurricane belt, so deadly storms are quite commonplace.

Seventy-five percent of the population is of combined Spanish and indigenous descent. The rest are either Europeans or descended from African slaves. Christianity, specifically the Catholic Church, is the state religion. Spanish is the official language.

Christopher Columbus named the island Hispaniola in 1492. Until that time, the sole inhabitants were Arawak people. Spain established the settlement of Santo Domingo as its main Caribbean base. Haiti, on the west of the island, was annexed by France in 1697. The whole island became French territory under the 1795 Treaty of Basel.

When Haiti became independent from France in 1804, it invaded the eastern region but was unsuccessful in attempts to impose control. Britain inter-ceded to impose peace following a rebellion in 1809. Spain resumed its control of the east. Haiti invaded again in 1821 and controlled the region until 1844.

The establishment of a republic in 1844 under President Pedro Santana provoked revolts by the people and another bloody conflict with Haiti. At Santana's request, the region became a Spanish province for four years.

The new leader, Buenaventura Báez, wrote a treaty, hoping to make the territory a part

Ice cream vendors in Santo Domingo.

of the United States. The U.S. Senate refused to ratify the agreement. Chaos followed. Ulíses Heureaux became dictator in 1882. His ruthless rule ended with his assassination in 1899.

The United States took control of the republic's finances following its bankruptcy in 1905. Civil disorder prompted the intervention of U.S. Marines. The military occupation lasted from 1916 to 1924.

After overthrowing President Horacio Vásquez in 1930, General Rafael Trujillo Molina established a brutal and ruthless dictatorship. He was assassinated in 1961. His replacement, President Joaquin Balaguer, was deposed in January of 1962. The Trujillo family became involved in various plan to regain control of the country.

Under the new constitution of December 1963, the first free election in forty years saw Juan Bosch elected president. He was deposed in a military coup only two years later. Civil war erupted in 1965 and led to Bosch's reinstatement. The Organization of American States (OAS) helped arrange a cease-fire.

In 1966 Balaguer was reelected with support from the Catholic Church. He was reelected again in 1970 and 1974 but defeated by Antonio Guzman in 1978. United States pressure prevented pro-Balaguer forces from staging a coup. Following Guzman's suicide four years later, Jacabo Majluta Azar became president.

Austerity measures imposed by the International Monetary Fund (IMF) generated widespread protests. Majluta was defeated by Balaguer for the presidency in 1986. Balaguer won again in 1990 as the country faced United States' allegations of involvement in the shipment of illegal narcotics.

The 1994 election was marked by massive electoral fraud by Balaguer, who was eighty-eight years old. Foreign economic aid being suspended and chaos followed once again. Dire economic conditions provoked widespread protests.

Leonel Fernández Reyna, a lawyer raised in New York, became president in 1996. His economic and social reforms were an attempt to overcome the worst of Balaguer's excesses.

Despite significant improvements, Fernández Reyna lost to the leftist candidate, Hipólito Mejía Dominguez, in 2000. Times have improved for the Dominican Republic, but it still has considerable work to do in in recovering from the damaging years of dictatorship.

GOVERNMENT
Website www.presidencia.gov.do
Capital Santo Domingo
Type of government Republic
Independence from Haiti
February 27, 1844
Voting Universal adult suffrage
Head of state President
Head of government President
Constitution 1966
Legislature
Bicameral National Congress
Chamber of Deputies (lower house),
Senate (upper house)
Judiciary Supreme Court
Member of
IMF, OAS, UN, UNESCO,
WHO, WTO

LAND AND PEOPLE
Land area 18,704 sq mi
(48,442 sq km)
Highest point Pico Duarte
10,287 ft (3175 m)
Coastline 823 mi (1288 km)
Population 8,721,594
Major cities and populations
Santo Domingo 1,600,000
Santiago de los Caballeros 370,000
San Francisco de Macoris 140,000
Ethnic groups
European-African 4%, European
15%, African 11%
Religions
Christianity 95%, others 1%
Languages Spanish (official)

ECONOMIC
Currency Dominican peso
Industry
tourism, sugar refining,
mining, textiles, cement
Agriculture
sugar cane, coffee, cotton, cacao,
rice, beans, potatoes, corn, bananas,
pigs, dairy, beef
Natural resources
nickel, bauxite, gold, silver

East Timor

REPUBLIC OF TIMOR LESTE

East Timor shares the island of Timor with Indonesia, which occupies the western half. It is located in the Lesser Sunda Islands group, between Java and Australia. The mountainous land runs roughly east-west. The climate is tropical, with hot and humid conditions throughout the year.

Most of the population is of Malay descent. Some are combined Malay and Portuguese, and there is a Papuan community. The population is overwhelmingly Christian. Portuguese is widely spoken, but East Timor is presently developing its own language.

Peoples from northern Asia settled in Timor as early as 3000 B.C. The Portuguese established a trading settlement in the sixteenth century. They were interested in the spices which grew in great abundance. The Dutch and British began laying claim to the island in 1613. Various struggles followed. The Dutch wanted Portugal claim confined to eastern Timor. Portugal agreed to the split in a 1859 treaty.

Japanese forces occupied the island during World War II. Timorese people assisted Allied commandos in a guerrilla war against the invaders. They were severely punished by the enemy.

Following the collapse of the Timor's Portuguese government in 1975, the Democratic Republic of East Timor was proclaimed. However, supported by the western powers, Indonesia forcibly annexed it.

For more than twenty years sporadic guerrilla activity required a large Indonesian army occupation. Prominent Timorese exiles attacked Indonesia's brutal occupation forces. Indonesian massacres and heavy-handed military actions brought the plight of East Timor into the international spotlight by the mid-1990s .

On August 30, 1999, East Timorese voted in a referendum to choose between independence and integration with Indonesia. Despite widespread intimidation of voters by Indonesian forces, the people voted for independence. Indonesia set its militia forces loose in a reign of terror and destruction. While the international community hesitated to send a peacekeeping force, much of the country was destroyed. Many people were massacred.

Finally, a United Nations force restored order, forcing the Indonesian militia out of East Timor. A United Nations group began rebuilding the country. On May 20, 2002, the Republic of East Timor came into being with former resistance leader Xanana Gusmao as president.

GOVERNMENT
Website www.gov.east-timor.org
Capital Dili
Type of government Republic
Independence from Indonesia May 20, 2002
Voting Universal adult suffrage
Head of state President
Head of government Prime Minister
Constitution 2002
Legislature Unicameral National Parliament
Judiciary Supreme Court of Justice
Member of IMF, UN

LAND AND PEOPLE
Land area 5,641 sq mi (14,609 sq km)
Highest point Foho Tatamailau 9,600 ft (2,963 m)
Coastline 440 mi (706 km)
Population 952,618
Major cities and populations Dili 160,000
Ethnic groups Malay, Papuan, Malay-Portuguese
Religions Christianity 90%, Islam 3%
Languages Tetum, Portuguese (both official)

ECONOMIC
Currency US dollar
Industry soap manufacturing, handicrafts, woven cloth
Agriculture coffee, rice, maize, cassava, sweet potatoes, soybeans, cabbage, mangoes, bananas, vanilla
Natural resources gold, petroleum, natural gas, manganese, marble